75¢

For
Father James Schall

The man who understands
the root of all evil

All the good wishes
of the authors

From the Publishers of the **Bond Buyer**

The Guide to Municipal Bonds: The History, The Industry, The Mechanics

by George J. Marlin and Joe Mysak

ISBN Number: 0-9618162-7-9

First Edition, 1991

Dedication

To

Dr. Larry Azar,
Professor of Philosophy,
Iona College

and

Susan Merett

.

Table of Contents

Preface

The Bond Buyer Guide to Municipal Bonds grew out of what we felt was a need in the market for a concise, readable primer on the business. It is aimed at people new to the field: students of public finance, newly-elected or appointed public officials, investors who want to know more than the yield and price of the issues they're buying, new hires on trading desks, fledgling investment bankers, and newspaper reporters assigned to cover local finance.

The *Guide* has something for all of these readers, and enough more to make it a worthy addition to any shelf of municipal market reference books. The book is structured to provide, first, an overview of the market, and then a look at how it operates.

In Chapter 1, the reader will find a comprehensive history of the municipal bond market from its origins in the earliest days of the Republic through the Tax Reform Act of 1986. The history of the market is the history of boom and bust economic cycles, and how municipalities rode out such storms. It is the history of the repudiation of Confederate state debt, of the Washington Public Power Supply System default, and of such diverse characters as Robert Moses, who showed politicians just what public authorities could do, and John Mitchell, now known primarily as a member of the Nixon White House but also the man who helped create the moral obligation bond.

The history of the municipal bond market features the almost constant fire of Congress and the Treasury upon the very concept of tax-exemption, considered by some to be the last bastion of state's rights, and of the ingenuity of bankers and issuers to overcome property tax caps and other limitations on a municipality's methods of financing everything from roads and bridges to schools and other public buildings.

Chapter 2 is a step by step examination of the general obligation, full faith and credit bond, including an in-depth look at an official statement, or offering prospectus, for a City of Chicago GO issue.

Revenue bonds, which now comprise almost three-quarters of the municipal market, are considered in Chapter 3. Do you need to find out the origin of the single-family mortgage revenue bond? Do you want to know what to look for before buying a hospital revenue bond? Are you considering the purchase of a university obligation, or a resource recovery bond? These are all analyzed in Chapter 3.

We then move on to the entire subject of the municipality, and how it finances its capital projects. Issuers can find a checklist of what to look for before going into the market, and a discussion of the advantages and disadvantages of negotiated or competitive financing.

The next two chapters walk the reader through actual deals, first competitive, where securities are put up for auction by sealed bid; then negotiated, where underwriters are chosen before the securities are marketed. The nuts and bolts of financing, from both an issuer's and an investor's perspective are described in Chapter 7. Such arcana as low-to-high, crossover and synthetic refundings are defined, as well as zero coupon bonds, tax-increment financings, variable-rate debt, leases, warrants, commercial paper programs and credit enhancement.

Chapter 9 covers the regulators in the market, what they do and what they have done, and ranges across the entire field of those who oversee the market, from trade groups to the U.S. Congress, and from bond counsel to the Municipal Securities Rulemaking Board.

Such is the formal text. The *Guide* contains three appendixes, the first on the history of *The Bond Buyer,* which was titled *The Daily Bond Buyer* from its founding in 1891 to 1982; the second on aspects of the Tax Reform Act of 1986; and the third on the rating agencies and their rating criteria and symbols. We conclude with a glossary of terms, the definitions running from a few words to a few hundred words as necessary.

Introduction

No matter what course tax reform takes, municipal financing is bound to increase in the 1990s. Cutbacks in federal aid, the historic 30-year cycle of infrastructure repair, and the demand for new housing and schools assures it.

The 1980s marked a sea change for municipal finance, with the market finishing its transition from one where the general obligation bond, sold at auction, was predominant, to one dominated by the revenue bond sold through negotiation. How this all happened is one of the major themes of this book.

Mr. Marlin, who has served as everything from a tax-exempt bond salesman to a portfolio manager, and Mr. Mysak, managing editor of the industry's daily newspaper, *The Bond Buyer*, which this year celebrated its centennial, take their readers through the history of the market and how it works. They cover everything from how to analyze a hospital bond, to how to choose a financial adviser, to how a trader can expect to spend his day.

They do so in a readable, nuts and bolts format accessible to even the general interest reader, refreshing in a day when so much of the work on the subject seems to have been written strictly for the academic and the analyst.

All those with a stake in municipal finance — bankers, investors, politicians, educators and journalists — would do well to know how the market works, why it works, and its history. This book is a great way to find out.

— William E. Simon

Acknowledgments

Like most books, this work has been enhanced thanks to the efforts of many friends and colleagues. The manuscript was carefully read and often improved by Brad Henderson, Michael G. Crofton and Thomas Flynn. To these people we owe a special debt.

At *The Bond Buyer*, very special thanks to President George Landgrebe; Joseph V. Riccobono, executive vice president and publisher; John H. Allan, editor of *The Bond Buyer;* and William J. Ryan, associate editor and market specialist. The staff of the newspaper has been of enormous help, including especially Rhonda Bennett, Jack Doran, Nick Boyle, Steve Dickson, Craig T. Ferris, Ted Hampton, Joan Pryde, Vicky Stamas, Lynn Stevens Hume and Dennis Walters.

Brad Henderson and George Yacik helped with the editing of the book, and Brian Sullivan brought this project back from the brink. Mary Margaret Frances McCartney helped keep a lot of this project on track.

Very special thanks to Kenneth J. McAlley, executive vice president and manager of the fixed income division at the United States Trust Company of New York. Also thanks to Joan Allman, Frank Butto, Michael G. Crofton, Lisa DePasquale, Gary Gildersleeve, Maria Illiano, Phyllis King, Phyllis Leonardi, Teresa Lorenzo, Rose McDonald, John McGrath, Henry Milkiwicz, Sandy Panetta, Charles Rabus and Terry Trought.

We are also grateful to the following, who were generous with their time and support: Catherine Barr, Richard Brookhiser, Florence D. Cohalan, Stanley D. Cornish, Andrew Ferguson, Brad Miner, Richard P. Rabatin, Mark L. Reed, Randy and Heather Richardson, George William Rutler, Jack Swan and William Wood.

Others in the municipal bond industry whose advice was sought include: Mike Ballinger, Ronald Carolanza, Gary Casino, Robert J. Collins, Michael Curley, Ronald Curvin, James C. Cusser, Joseph Darden, Sylvan G. Feldstein, Ronald Fromm, Joseph Hickey, J. Chester and Freda Johnson, Michael Kean, Austin V. Koenen, Gregory Miles, Brian O'Connor, Michael P. O'Daly, Gerald Orefice, Stephen P.

Rappaport, Donald B. Scalley, Hon. William E. Simon, Louis Sprauer, Christopher Sweeny, Austin J. Tobin, Jon Tumler, Robert Weiland, James Wilson and Charles G. Woram.

Also, thanks to the Marlins in the municipal bond business: William M. Marlin, James P. Marlin, Barbara D. Marlin, Dennis Marlin, Scott Marlin and Maureen Marlin.

Finally, thanks to our old friend Harry Poulakakos of Harry's at Hanover Square for providing the table where the idea for this book germinated.

A note on the glossary: With all works like this, we owe a debt to those who have gone before us. Our glossary would not have been possible without the study of such excellent sources as the Municipal Securities Association's *Glossary of Municipal Bond Terms*, Lennox L. Moak's *Municipal Bonds: Planning, Sale, and Administration*, and the Public Securities Association's *Fundamentals of Municipal Bonds* among others.

We are grateful to all those who kindly helped us. Any inaccuracies are our own.

George J. Marlin
Joe Mysak
The City of New York
June 25, 1991

Chapter 1:

Municipal Finance: A Historic Overview

New York City: The Cycles of Financial Excess

The Governor of the State of New York entered the press room and began the news conference.

"At an all-day session between the city officials and representatives of the banks, which followed a number of other conferences in the past 10 days, a comprehensive plan for the financing of the City of New York and for unemployment relief was formulated," he said. "The plan met with the tentative approval of all present.

"The plan will be submitted tomorrow for approval to the Board of Estimate and Apportionment and to the banks of the city. If the plan is accepted by both parties, it is likely that legislation by the state legislature will be necessary to make effective some of its provisions. I have advised the city officials and the bankers that if this is the case I will call an extraordinary session of the legislature, but only after the proposed legislation, in definite form, has been agreed upon by the legislative leaders of both parties."

With these words, Gov. Herbert Lehman initiated a program that saved New York City from financial default and bankruptcy in September 1933. His words could just as easily have been uttered by Gov. Hugh Carey in 1975 when the city again faced financial collapse.

The Greater City of New York, the "Imperial City" as 1924 Democratic presidential candidate James McAdoo labeled it, reflects and magnifies the nation's history of public finance, both its achievements and its failures. New York City floated the first general obligation bond in 1812, and for most of the municipal bond market's history was its dominant issuer. It frequently led the way in developing public finance techniques — many revenue bonds and public authorities were created to accommodate the needs of the nation's largest city. There is also a darker side to New York's history — political corruption and ideological excess — that led to the abuse of the municipal market and of tax-exempt financing.

The city of bright lights, champagne and silk hats was the New York of the 1920s. British journalist G.K. Chesterton, walking down Broadway for the first time in 1921, proclaimed, "What a glorious garden of wonders this would be to anyone who was lucky enough to be unable to read." New York exuded what all admired of the Jazz Age, and its mayor, "Beau" Jimmy Walker, personified the excesses of the era. James J. Walker charmed the citizenry with his wit and style and ran the government from speakeasies and night clubs.

During the Walker era, the Tammany Hall bosses reigned supreme; municipal corruption and political nepotism flourished. Questioned about a particular incompetent he appointed to the Children's Court, Walker replied, "The children will now be judged by one of their peers."

In the fall of 1931, the Joint Legislative Committee, in investigating the affairs of the City of New York, met in Manhattan's County Courthouse. The Chief Counsel, Judge Samuel Seabury , began to question Thomas M. Farley, Sheriff of New York County, leader of the 14th Assembly District and Tammany Hall sachem. Farley was asked to explain how in six years he managed to save $400,000, while his annual salary was only $5,000. The following exchange ensued:

Seabury: Where did you keep these moneys that you had saved?

Farley: In a safe-deposit box at home in the house.

Seabury: Whereabouts at home in the house did you keep this money that you had saved?

Farley: In the safe.

Seabury: In the safe?

Farley: Yes.

Seabury: In a little box in a safe?

Farley: A big safe.

Seabury: But a little box in a big safe?

Farley: In a big box in a big safe.

Seabury: Now, in 1930, where did the extra cash come from, Sheriff?

Farley: Well, that is —, my salary check is in there.

Seabury: No, Sheriff, your salary checks are exclusive of the cash deposits which during the year you deposited in those three banks.

Farley: Well, that came from the good box I had. (Laughter.)

Seabury: Kind of a magic box?

Farley: It was a wonderful box.

Seabury: A wonderful box. (Laughter) What did you have to do —rub the lock with a little gold, and open it in order to find more money?

Farley: I wish I could.

Thus began the decline of Jimmy Walker. New Yorkers grew weary of their cheerleader, and at the height of the 1932 Seabury corruption investigations, the King of the Jazz Era abdicated the office of mayor.

Upon ascending office, Mayor John P. O'Brien, Walker's successor, immediately recognized that as a result of budget padding and declining revenues, the city bordered on bankruptcy. For years, public officials issued short-term debt and raided capital project funds, sinking funds and pension funds to cover up the deficits. In addition, there were the economic consequences of the Depression — between 1930 and 1932, revenues declined by $50 million while expenditures jumped $100 million. O'Brien implemented cuts, but it was too little, too late. In 1933, with little investor confidence, the banks refused to underwrite additional debt.

Investment bankers, led by Thomas Lamont of J.P. Morgan & Co., eventually cut a deal with Gov. Lehman and city leaders. Wall Street agreed to supply short-term cash advances, underwrite some debt refundings and issue securities backed by a revolving fund. The city's end of the bargain consisted of promises to create budget reserves, to segregate and deposit tax collections in the banks, and to withdraw proposals to increase taxes on savings banks, insurance companies and property.

In January 1934, reformer Fiorello LaGuardia took over City Hall, imposed stringent budget cuts, and nursed New York back to financial health.

During his first term, LaGuardia lifted the city from financial and spiritual lows. He balanced the budget and implemented a sales tax. His congressional experience and cordial relationship with President Franklin D. Roosevelt gave him the inside track to procure a hugely disproportionate share of federal funds for jobs, housing, parks, subway cars and bridges. And his greatest achievement, the development of municipal civil service based on merit and objective selection, destroyed the patronage base of the bosses of Tammany.

Many observers proclaimed LaGuardia the greatest mayor in New York City's history, and in 1937 he was reelected easily. Yet, he lost his zest for the job because, in his mind, he had brought "the city as far along the path of modernity as possible." His ambitions and attention turned toward Washington, for he now pictured himself as the successor to FDR.

His absentee stewardship began to take its toll. "Petty corruption crept into the administration through the cracks of LaGuardia's disinterest," in the words of one author. With federal dollars being diverted from the cities to fund the war effort, New York City faced serious budget problems. The mayor began to use "questionable accounting schemes to cover the services he introduced, and comptroller Joseph McGoldrick was dismissing deficits as entirely a bookkeeping transaction as he switched current expenses from tax levy funds to bonded debt."

"The city faces a crisis in its fiscal affairs," the Citizens Budget Commission announced shortly after the 1941 election, detailing the price that the city was paying for its modern, caring government. In 15 years, annual city expenditures, exclusive of emergency unemployment relief, had grown three times more rapidly than the city population, while the debt multiplied five and a half times population growth. Over and above a 210% increase in federal and state contributions, city expenditures advanced by more than 40%, while gross bonded debt doubled.

Rather than accept this as the price of good intentions and large government, LaGuardia used every possible fiscal artifice to hide the full cost of his progressive urban policies. During the war, LaGuardia took advantage of the forced savings produced by the war economy (supply shortages prevented some expenditures that had already been approved and budgeted, and the draft pulled a large number of civil servants off the salary rolls) to camouflage growing municipal costs. Then he still overspent. Came the end of the year, when the city was behind in its receipts, comptroller McGoldrick would roll over its bills to the next year's budget. *Brooklyn Eagle* columnist William Heffernan referred to the camouflaged budget as "the final stage of a municipal rake's progress . . . the gimme philosophy raised to the nth degree, the legacy of a 'government that has spent without discretion and taxed without care.' "

The investment banking firm of Lazard Freres and Co. declared in a credit report that the city lacked "proper retrenchment in expenditures for both current and capital purposes." The city insisted on expanding government services; yet as the Citizens Budget Commission pointed out, the programs rested on an "insubstantial fiscal foundation."

Historian Thomas Kessner concluded: "By the time he [La Guardia] left office, the city had been transformed into the colossal metropolis; it was saddled with debt, an infrastructure too expensive to maintain comfortably, dangerously expanding citizen expectations, and snowballing bureaucracy."

The post-war boom helped lift the city from its fiscal malaise. However, during this period, the ideological seeds were planted that eventually destroyed its financial base.

It was Mayor Robert F. Wagner who expressed the political view that prevailed in the 1950s, 1960s and early 1970s. He stated: "I do not propose to permit our fiscal problems to set the limits of our commitments to meet the essential needs of the people of the city." This philosophy and various federal and state decisions eventually led to the distorted revenue estimates and rollovers that once again closed the financial community's door to the city. It also led to the situation where by 1975, 25 types of taxes supported 19 municipal hospitals, day care centers and foster homes, a tuition-free City University system, and over one million people on welfare.

The November 1961 City Charter revisions granted Mayor Wagner absolute power to estimate general fund revenues. Recognizing the significance of this change, the Citizen's Budget Commission reported: "When you had a Mayor operating with a Budget Bureau which was creative, the sky was the limit. There were no checks. You had creative budget officials playing the fifth violin, the piccolo and the kettle drum all by themselves."

The sanctioning of budgetary abuses continued throughout the 1960s and 1970s. In 1964, the New York State Legislature amended Chapter 284, Section 2, of the Local Finance Law, permitting the city to place general fund expenditures into the capital budget. Additional changes in the Finance Law (1967) allowed "the costs of codification laws and fees paid to experts, lawyers and consultants, advertising and costs of printing and dissemination" to be included in the capital project funds. The rationale was that they had a three-year period of probable usefulness.

Taking advantage of these loopholes, Mayor John V. Lindsay in 1968 transferred $84 million of the city's general fund expenditures to the capital budget. By 1975, that figure proliferated to $835 million — more than half of the capital projects budget.

During this period, the mayor also received the authority to issue revenue anticipation notes based on his own "guesstimates" and *not* on the actual receipts of the previous fiscal year. In 1971, the city began issuing budget notes to cover distorted revenue estimates — $300 million were issued in 1971, $400 million in 1972. There was apparently no intention of paying them off; they were just rolled into new borrowings.

Succumbing to the demands of the Civil Service, unions also contributed to the city's demise. In March 1958, Mayor Wagner signed an executive order that permitted over 100,000 city employees to join unions and to hold collective bargaining sessions. By 1977, 98% of the city's employees belonged to unions. Bureau of the Budget figures reveal that between 1960 and 1975, wages jumped 31.6%. This was substantially greater than salary gains in the private sector and the inflation rate. Retirement at half pay after 20 years' service, granted to the police in 1957, was granted to almost every municipal union. The Committee for Economic Development observed that between 1960 and 1970, New York State enacted 54 city pension bills. Retirement costs, according to the Temporary Commission on City Finances, rose more than 600% (from $206 million to $1.48 billion) during the period 1961 to 1976, and unfunded pension liabilities hit $8 billion by 1977.

Budgetary gimmicks, phantom revenues and capitalizing of expenses led to a situation where in 1975 city expenditures totalled $12.8 billion and revenues $10.9 billion. Fifty-six percent of locally raised taxes were appropriated for debt service, pension and social security payments. In addition, short-term debt, which in 1965 was $536 million (10% of total debt), ballooned to $4.5 billion (36% of total debt) by 1975. With 1976 short-term debt needs projected at $7 billion, the financial markets closed their doors to New York City.

Reforming the City

In his book *The Bankers*, Martin Mayer wrote:
"On the simplest level, the story of New York's financial collapse is the tale of a Ponzi game in municipal paper — the regular and inevitably increasing issuance of notes to be paid off not by future taxes or revenue certified to be available for that purpose, but by the sale of future notes. Like all chain-

letter swindles, Ponzi games self-destruct when the seller runs out of suckers, as New York did in spring 1975."

New York was brought to its knees because of its huge permanent short-term debt. Viewing the mess, journalist Ken Auletta declared, "The rollovers, false revenue estimates and plain lies have robbed the taxpayers of literally billions through excessive borrowings to cover-up excessive fraud."

Gov. Hugh Carey, grasping the magnitude of the situation, forced the city to begin internal reforms. In a September 1975 message to an emergency session of the state legislature, he stated: "In the hope that further drastic reforms of the city's internal financing and management structure would restore the financial community's and the public's confidence in the city, far-reaching steps were taken or agreed to by the city, in close consultation with the State and [the recently formed Municipal Assistance Corp. for the City of New York] to improve its condition, including:

— the formation of a Management Advisory Committee to assist in streamlining the city's management;

—a ceiling on the size of the city's budget;

— a moratorium on additional taxes;

— dismissal of thousands of municipal workers, elimination of thousands of positions from the city's budget, and a freeze on new hiring;

— a suspension of wage increases of city employees;

— an increase in public transit fare;

— a further reduction in the budget of the City University and an increase in student fees that endangers its long-standing free tuition policy;

— a significant reduction of the capital budget

— appointment of a special mayoral deputy for finance."

These measure were not enough to restore investor confidence, and in November 1975 the city defaulted by decree of the state legislature. Moratorium legislation was enacted on $2.6 billion of notes. Holders of the paper were offered 10-year 8% MAC bonds in place of principal payments.

The city went to Washington and exerted tremendous pressure for a federal bailout, but U.S. Treasury Secretary William E. Simon held firm, insisting that the federal government "should offer no help to New York until and unless a powerful commitment was first made to adopt a responsible fiscal program." New York capitulated to Washington's demands, and in December 1975 President Ford signed legislation permitting short-term loans up to $2.3 billion a year.

To regain access to the credit markets, New York City was forced to overhaul its governing institutions. Those reforms will help prevent another financial disaster for the city.

The offices of the mayor and comptroller developed sophisticated accounting, reporting, forecasting and internal control systems. In *American Cities and the New York Experience,* Charles Brecher and Raymond Horton commented: "The city has improved its information systems and integrated them into a financial planning process with a long-term perspective. The city that literally did not know how many people it employed in 1975 now projects staffing levels, borrowing, and cash flow for four-year periods, and has a 10-year plan for capital investments. The system...is probably one of the best management information systems among large American cities and rivals the practices of well-managed private firms."

The internal reforms certainly enhanced New York's credibility, and the various entities created to supervise the city will help stifle any temptation by elected officials to backslide. The Municipal Assistance Corp., the Office of the Special Deputy Comptroller for New York City, and the Emergency Financial Control Board are all overseers of the city's financial process.

The control board, the most powerful of the supervisory institutions, actually has absolute authority over city finances. This body, which will exist for the life of MAC bonds, can dictate to the mayor not only the amount of budget cuts, but where those cuts will be made. It can reject financial plans, scheduled borrowings, and municipal union contracts. If all else fails, this board will help save the city from financial collapse.

But these events did not immediately curtail outrageous spending habits. Tremendous deficits were still tolerated; $1.1 billion in 1976 and $1 billion in 1977. It took Mayor Edward I. Koch's hardball approach to finances and the effects of Reaganomics to bring the city into the black. Certain mechanics were put in place to avoid future debacles.

Although it is conceivable the city's political and economic conditions will deteriorate in the 1990s, it is unlikely New Yorkers will witness the financial antics employed in the past. This is because in 1975 the city's old political ringleaders relinquished major aspects of home rule to its private and public creditors and their fiscal monitors.

Some Common Problems

It is fair to say that since the end of the Second World War, every U.S. city has faced some aspect of the problems that confronted New York City in 1975. Indeed, some political scientists believe that it is nothing less than a political cycle, "embedded in the conception of U.S. cities as competitive firms: They must justify themselves both in polling booths and in capital markets," in the words of Seymour J. Mandelbaum in his study, *Boss Tweed's New York.*

Mandelbaum, discussing another study of the rise and fall of New York City in the 1970s, noted, "In this cycle, the periodic creation of a fiscal crisis allows elite groups to discipline democratic demands for services. . . . Bankers and bondholders manufacture a 'crisis' leading to fiscal and social contraction before budgetary constraints were relaxed in a new round of 'politics as usual' which responded to long-delayed demands for infrastructure investments, jobs, and services."

New York City, then, may represent the cyclical nature of municipal finance and the development of the tax-exempt bond industry.

Bankruptcy and Default

New York City did indeed default on its municipal debt in 1975. When holders of its notes presented them at maturity for principal and interest, they were not given cash; instead they received new bonds. Insiders prefer to call this a technical default.

To date, there have been a little over $6 billion in recorded municipal defaults, far less than 1% of total outstanding tax-exempt debt. The story of bond defaults centers around the various economic cycles during the first 150 years of our nation's history. With the exception of the 1930's Great Depression, revenue bond failures predominated in parts of the country under development.

The first economic cycle witnessed debt being floated for municipal waterworks, canals, turnpikes and railroads. The depression of 1837 brought this expansion to a halt, and over

50% of outstanding debt went under, including debt sold by nine states: Arkansas, Florida, Illinois, Indiana, Louisiana, Maryland, Michigan, Mississippi and Pennsylvania. State legislatures reacted to the crisis by passing constitutional amendments that prohibited their states from issuing long-term debt, forcing them to implement pay-as-you-go financing.

By the 1860s, state tax-exempt debt expanded rapidly to finance expenses incurred during the Civil War. Local debt began to grow to finance railroad expansion and peaked in 1870 when outstanding local municipal debt stood at $516 million; the accumulated debt of the states totaled $353 million.

When the depression of 1873-1879 hit, numerous land schemes and speculation frauds were revealed. A.M. Hillhouse, in his 1936 classic, *Municipal Bonds: A Century of Experience,* excerpts from a typical prospectus the optimistic expectations:

"Were the company to purchase a million of acres of the lands adjacent to the work, the increase alone in the price of the lands so purchased would, before the work is half completed, pay for the entire construction of the work. The bare location of the route would triple the price of every acre of land within two miles of it. All that is wanted is capital to invest in the lands, and to go on with the work for a short time without being compelled to make sale of them."

Two-thirds of all the debt issued on behalf of railroads defaulted during that depression; the other third was debt repudiated by the former Confederate States of America. In 1897, *The Daily Bond Buyer* reported that during the 1870s, the former Southern states had repudiated more than $250 million in bonds sold mainly for the construction of railroads and levees. Most of them subsequently made settlements with bondholders on such debt, for varying amounts.

At the end of the Reconstruction Era, the governments of the Southern states walked away from debt incurred by "carpet-baggers," those Northern politicians who moved in after the war and who routinely robbed municipalities with padded costs to repair wartorn waterworks, housing and civic structures. In Columbia, South Carolina, a city counsel member summed up the situation:

"I was a member of the council for a part of the war time, and as chairman of the Ways and Means Committee, had become familiar with its financial condition. On declining to serve, after a re-election, I publicly expressed the opinion that by proper management, with increased but not immoderate taxation for three or four years, and the sale of the city's $150,000 in stock of the Greenville and the Charlotte Railroads, the entire bonded debt of $320,000 might be paid off and the citizens freed from future taxation except for current expenses. The overthrow of the Confederacy and the destruction of the place by Sherman, of course, prevented any attempt at proving the correctness of my opinion. But the Radical party then took charge of the municipality, and in the face of the facts that the city had been desolated, as already described, and that its people were just crawling out of the ashes, as if determined to defeat our exertions for returning prosperity, they engaged in the wildest schemes of useless extravagance and waste. . . . "

Municipal debt throughout the remainder of the 19th century and into the 20th century continued to grow after each depression. History repeated itself during the economic downturn of the 1890s, when 30% of the defaults were railroad-related.

Municipal debt, which stood at $2 billion in 1900, increased to $12.8 billion by 1928. This increase may be attributed to the population influx to America's major urban centers, roadbuilding to accommodate the automobile, and the rise of suburbia and its essential service requirements.

Those growing areas that incurred the most debt naturally suffered the most during the Great Depression of the 1930s.

Between 1929 and 1933, 4,770 local municipalities defaulted on $2.85 billion of debt; in 1933, more than 16% of the market was in default. Property taxes and their corresponding tax bases took nose dives. By the 1940s, almost all of these defaults were cleared up, and observers have stated that they were cleared up mainly because 95% of all debt at the time was general obligation, backed by the full faith and credit of the issuing municipality. They point out that today, the majority of the bonds issued are revenue bonds, without full faith and credit backing, which paints a much bleaker credit picture for any sustained economic downturn.

Municipal bond historian A.M. Hillhouse, looking over the period 1800-1937, came up with 26 reasons why defaults occurred. The following summarizes his conclusions:

A. Defaults have occurred on every type of bond, but water and school bonds are least affected.

B. Defaults have occurred in all sections of the country, but the South and Midwest were hit the hardest due to the Civil War and rapid expansion.

C. The bulk of defaults occurred during depressions.

D. Losses to bondholders have been negligible. Although the greatest losses were on railroad bonds, remedies during that era were developed by a federal judiciary sympathetic to creditors' interests.

E. Defaults were generally the result of the heavy accumulation of fixed debt service costs during boom periods and breakdowns in the municipal structures during depressions.

F. Most defaults were due to real estate speculation and the ensuing overborrowing.

Several notable studies of municipal bond defaults have been published. Chief among them are George Hempel's several works on "The Postwar Quality of Municipal Bonds," used by most of the major municipal bond insurers for their underwriting standards; Robert Godfrey's *Risk-Based Capital Charges for Municipal Bonds,* published in 1990; and Enhance Reinsurance Co.'s very useful "Municipal Default Patterns."

The Role of Chapter 9 Bankruptcy

Bridgeport, Conn., made headlines in 1991 when it became the first major city to file for Chapter 9 bankruptcy protection. The city of almost 140,000 was the largest municipality ever to file for Chapter 9 and sparked worries among some observers that such filings would be the wave of the future. It also sparked hope among others that here, at last, was a way for cities to turn out the rascals in charge and tame organized labor.

The city's filing was contested by the state, which contended that Bridgeport had no authority to take such an action, but the episode spoke volumes about the perilous condition of certain municipalities. To be sure, the recession in late 1990 and early 1991was not kind to them. At the time, more than half of the states were running in the red, with several looking at deficits unseen before —New York State, for example, was experiencing a deficit of more than $4 billion, while Connecticut faced a $2 billion gap.

And it got bleaker below the state level, as cities and counties scrambled to make up for revenues that significantly lagged spending. Philadelphia, perhaps the most notorious case, had been flirting with insolvency for five months, and only recently had managed to close a financing deal designed to give it a few months of breathing room, albeit with a loan whose annualized true interest cost approached almost 25%. In New York, Gov. Mario Cuomo threatened to reconvene the Financial Control Board, idle since the mid-1980s, to oversee New York City's ailing finances. And in Colorado, a handful of special districts set up when boom times still beckoned actually went into bankruptcy in the fall of 1990.

"It's definitely an option to be looked at," one lawyer said of Chapter 9 protection. But looking is one thing. Taking the leap is another. At least part of the problem is that Chapter 9, which is reserved for states and their subdivisions, is largely misunderstood, even by those consultants who sell their expertise to municipalities as financial advisers and bond counsel. Said one financial adviser, "There are countervailing interests to abrogation of debt and abrogation of contracts." Another noted, "A municipality sells full faith and credit debt, saying it will tax whatever it takes to pay that debt. Chapter 9 is a renunciation of that commitment and represents a failure of political will. Whatever short-term gains there are will be wiped out by the market's memory. The issuer loses credence in the eyes of bond buyers. And there is no question that the democratic process will be subverted."

Such "expertise" — almost all of which is misguided — may in fact be the reason why more localities do not avail themselves of Chapter 9. Bankruptcy is apparently not even in the vocabulary of most experts, so conscious are they of the historical opprobrium attached to it.

Yet the taint attached to municipal bankruptcy was supposedly done away with in 1988, when Chapter 9, which dates from 1937, was amended. Under the original law, a municipality's bondholders were treated much like the rest of its creditors, of which 51% had to approve any municipality's move into Chapter 9. Revenue dedicated to repayment of a municipality's revenue bonds could be diverted from bondholders to other purposes, thus changing the bondholders from creditors with rights to specifically identified revenues into general creditors. In addition, interest paid on any of the municipality's bonds could be reclaimed within 90 days of the bankruptcy filing, the same as a corporate bankrupt's.

In sum, under the old law, there was very little protection for a municipality's revenue bond holders. This led to the stigma that seriously impaired any municipality's future ability to enter the bond market once it emerged from Chapter 9. As James E. Spiotto, a partner at the Chicago law firm of Chapman & Cutler, wrote in support of the 1988 amendments, "The only way to avoid the stigma of a Chapter 9 proceeding in the municipal bond market is to assure that the statutory and constitutional pledges and rights granted to bondholders remain in effect during the Chapter 9 proceeding."

Demonstrating municipalities' sensitivity to market perception is the way that most of them, even under the old Chapter 9, ignored the provision terminating their special pledges, and carefully avoided tapping dedicated revenues. A case in point was the San Jose, Calif., school district, which was forced into Chapter 9 in 1983, mainly because of high teacher wages. The district made it clear in its filing that bondholders were not parties to the bankruptcy, and continued making principal and interest payments on its bonds throughout the proceeding. Bankruptcy may be forever in the corporate market, where it frequently represents ruined dreams. But in the municipal market, it might only be a heartbeat.

The new Chapter 9, which protects revenue bond holders, is clear on this point of bankruptcy. And it is clear on a number of other points in which it differs significantly from Chapter 11 corporate bankruptcy. For one thing, Chapter 9 is voluntary; creditors cannot put a municipality, no matter how ill-managed, into bankruptcy. For another, a municipality must be specifically authorized to proceed into Chapter 9 — many states, conscious of the shame of insolvency, prohibit it outright. And for a third, municipal bankruptcy is less a means designed to shut down or reorganize a municipality than it is for that municipality to adjust its debt load — but almost never its *bonded* indebtedness. The municipality still must function as a municipality, providing vital services like police and fire protection, water and electricity. Under the 10th amendment, the courts handling the bankruptcy are forbidden from interfering with the fiscal, governmental or even political affairs of the municipality, including impairment of contractual obligations.

And this includes, or could include, labor contracts, another specific area where municipal and corporate bankruptcy part ways. In a 1984 case, *National Labor Relations Board v. Bildisco and Bildisco,* the Supreme Court held that, with certain exceptions, a trustee may assume or reject collective bargaining agreements. James Spiotto, who is the foremost authority on municipal bankruptcy, has written, "Given the fact that labor obligations are among the most burdensome problems faced by municipalities" — Bridgeport's 14 union contracts account for 60% of its budget, for example, while Philadelphia's labor costs take up over half of its budget — "the Bildisco result obviously could be attractive to some local governments. However, municipal workers generally perform a governmental function. It is not clear, then, whether the Bildisco holding would govern a municipal bankruptcy. Absent a resolution by the debtor municipality's legislative body approving or disproving rejection, the provisions . . . of the Code require that the Bankruptcy Court cannot interfere with the political or governmental powers of the debtor. Accordingly, the jurisdiction of the Bankruptcy Court is limited, and the termination of a labor contract contrary to the wishes of the municipality's elected officials may be subject to attack as beyond the court's power."

With most experts lacking the knowledge of just what is and what is not involved in a municipal bankruptcy, then, it seems likely that Chapter 9 will continue to be used by those who have always favored it: the small and desperate. "In fact, it represents an option for a number of smaller, local units" like villages and water and school districts, in the words of one banker. "The bigger you get, a certain momentum develops against it."

The fact is, unlike the early wild and woolly days of municipal finance, when scores of municipalities scouted for *ultra vires* ways to repudiate their debt — saying they never had the legal ability to sell bonds — modern municipalities would rather do almost anything, even default, than go into Chapter 9. There have been thousands of corporate bankruptcies since 1937, but there have only been around 400 cases of municipal bankruptcy — and this scattered among the roughly 80,000 municipal entities in existence.

It may be easier, physically, nowadays to enter bankruptcy. But it is still not seen, psychologically, as an option by major issuers. This probably has more to do with the old-fashioned nature of the market than anything else. After all, not too many years ago, an issuer refunding its high-coupon debt was looked upon as not exactly sporting.

Will there be a rash of municipal bankruptcies? Fiscal conditions seem to favor it; even the National Association of Bond Lawyers said it expected Chapter 9 filings to "become more of a reality" in the coming years. But a rash in the municipal market is a minor irritation to the rest of the world, and should be seen that way. Twenty municipal bankruptcies would in fact represent an absolute wave of Chapter 9 filings.

Instead, it seems likely that we can look for the municipal bond market to deal with its basket cases and transgressors in the way it always has. For those municipalities which have experienced a cash shortfall through little fault of their own, there will be a sharpening of the budget axe and some chiding by the bond rating agencies. For those with more serious problems, there will be higher taxes, deficit bonds and short-term notes, and political upheaval. For those in even more dire condition, there will be state loans, issuance of state-guaranteed debt, and loss of political power over budgets to oversight agencies like New Jersey's Municipal Finance Commission or New York's Financial Control Board.

As for those troublesome labor contracts, most municipal union chiefs are fast learning that when they demand raises, they should also be willing to accept layoffs and increased productivity clauses. A union member with a raise is a content union member, while a union member without a job is an ex-member without a vote at the next union election.

Chapter 9 has a role to play in municipal finance, but the fundamental restructuring of the municipal market's sick men always will take place long before the decision to file for bankruptcy is reached.

Revenue Bonds and the Rise of Authorities

The post-World War II era witnessed increased demands on local governments and tremendous growth in bonded debt. Defaults continued, but consistent with past history, they generally occurred with revenue bonds backed by private entities, as in the case of hospital and industrial development bonds.

The biggest default was on $2.25 billion of debt by the Washington Public Power Supply System in 1983. As New York City tells the story of GO bonds, WPPSS tells the story of Murphy's law applied to revenue supported tax-exempt debt. But first a background on the history of revenue bonds and the major figures who contributed to that development is essential.

In the early years of the republic, the belief that the public treasury should be raided to support specialized projects was rejected. The revenue bond concept was implemented to permit public services to be paid by those who used the facility. Most revenue bonds issued in the 1800s were for water supply systems, and were also backed by the general obligation of the issuing public entity. It was not until 1885 when Wheeling, West Virginia, formalized the position that principal and interest on water works bonds should come exclusively from the project's earnings.

A bond ordinance of that city, relating to the financing of a combined water and gas plant, went as far as it could in this direction under then-existing legal restrictions:

"Inasmuch as it is not permitted by the constitution and laws of the state to provide for the redemption of bonds to be issued under this ordinance otherwise than by a levy of direct annual taxes, and it is intended in the adoption of this loan ordinance not to cause any increase in the direct taxation; therefore, to provide as far as possible against any such increase, it is further ordained that there shall be paid into the city treasury from the revenue of the city water works and gas works . . . an amount equal to the annual interest on the unredeemed portion of this loan outstanding, and from 1895 to 1919 a sum annually equal to one twenty-fifth of the principal of the loan."

Over the years, the concept of the pure revenue bond expanded, and the purposes expanded to include the building of everything from armories and bridges to sanitariums, golf courses and swimming pools.

Chicago in 1898 attempted to float its first revenue bond, for water supply, only to be stopped by the judicial system, which ruled that such an issue must have the backing of the city's general obligation pledge. It took Chicago seven years to receive the approval of the state legislature to issue bonds whose sole backing was users ' fees.

The first state revenue bond was issued in 1920. Kentucky approved financing that was secured by a first lien on State

Fair property. The principal and interest was payable out of State Board of Agriculture income. In 1924, Oklahoma issued revenue bonds payable from income received by the State University dormitories and the Agriculture and Mechanical College.

The most important development in the history of the revenue bond was the 1921 Act of the New York and New Jersey legislatures that created the Port Authority of New York and New Jersey. The act, which was also approved by the U.S. Congress, was copied from the 300-year old Port of London Authority. It was so titled because the Act of Parliament that defined its powers began with the phrase "Authority is hereby given..." The new agency sold $34 million in bonds in 1926.

The actions of the Port Authority were a milestone in the history of municipal finance: the agency issued the largest amount of revenue bonds to date; they were for a new type of project — toll bridges; and the bonds were to finance multiple projects. In the past, authorities had a mandate to create only one project, and after the bonds were paid off, title of the project reverted to the municipality. The authority would cease to exist and the upkeep of the edifice would be the responsibility of the municipality. But the Port Authority was given a longer life because its indenture permitted the building of several projects.

During this period there arrived on the scene a man who was destined to have an incredible impact on municipal finance and was to be recognized as the greatest builder of public works since the Pharoahs. His name: Robert Moses.

The Master Builder: Robert Moses

Born in New Haven in 1888, Robert Moses was educated at Yale and Oxford. After completing his Ph.D. in Public Administration, he joined the Bureau of Municipal Research, a think tank located in New York City.

Recognized as a visionary, he was without power until he befriended Gov. Alfred E. Smith. With his appointment by Smith as president of the Long Island State Park Commission, Moses began building an empire of agencies and activities that was to overshadow elected officials for half a century.

His reputation as an innovator who could implement his dreams was cemented in the minds of the general public when he broke up the great estates and polo fields of Long Island to build a recreational center for the common man — Jones Beach. But his greatest impact on municipal finance stemmed from his chairmanship of the Triborough Bridge Authority and his interpretation of the entity's ability to incur bonded debt.

Biographer Robert Caro, in his masterful biography of Moses, *The Power Broker*, describes Moses' early traditional approach to authorities and their bonded debt: "Originally, he had conceived of his authorities in the traditional mold: the legislation he had drafted establishing the Triborough, Henry Hudson, and Marine Parkway bodies, for example, has explicitly authorized each to construct only a single, specific project and to issue bonds only for that project; the bonds were to be paid off as soon as possible, and not only was a time limit (40 years) set on their expiration but that time limit also limited the authority's life — as soon as its bonds were paid off, it was to go out of existence and turn over its bridge to the city government. "

When he accepted the chairmanship, the impact of the Depression made the completion of the Triborough Bridge appear unlikely. The current view that New York City was a series of islands that could not cope with its ever-growing automobile traffic looked as though it would prevail for the foreseeable future. Moses, however, managed to put together the finances and created four separate bridges that linked three boroughs: Queens, the Bronx and Manhattan.

The unexpected financial success of the bridges began to change Moses' thinking on the purpose of public authorities. The total principal and interest payments and maintenance costs for the Henry Hudson Bridge, for example, was approximately $425,000 a year. After these expenditures, net income in 1938 was $600,000. With net surpluses increasing every year, the bonds would be paid off, not in 40 years, but in eight or nine years. The financial situation was the same at all the other bridges — toll collections were substantially larger than annual expenditures.

Moses did not want to lose his power base by putting his authorities out of business, nor did he want to lose control of the surplus dollars. He needed to change state law and Moses, reputed to be the best bill drafter in Albany, launched a plan that would forever change the face of municipal finance.

As Caro wrote: "Authorities could issue bonds. A bond was simply a legal agreement between its seller and buyer. A legal agreement was, by definition, a contract. And under the Constitution of the United States, a contract was sacred. No state — and no creature of a state such as a city — could impair its obligations. No one — not Governor, not Mayor, not State Legislature, not City Board of Estimate — could interfere with its provisions. If Robert Moses could write the powers which had been vested in him into the bond contracts of his authorities, make those powers parts of the agreements under which investors purchased the bonds, those powers would be his for as long as the authorities should remain in existence and he should control them. If he could keep the authorities in existence indefinitely and could keep his place at their head, he would hold those powers indefinitely — quite conceivably, until he died. "

Moses knew he could not eliminate many of the safeguards found in the Triborough Bridge Authority's indenture; instead, he made them worthless. Here are his innocuous insertions into the authority's enabling legislation:

1) "The authority shall have power from time to time to refund any bonds by the issuance of new bonds, whether the bonds to be refunded have or have not matured, and may issue bonds partly to refund bonds then outstanding and partly for any other corporate purpose."

That line permitted Moses to issue 40-year bonds that could be refunded every 39 years. The effect would be that Moses could start building all over again with the proceeds. He would no longer have to pay the bonds off in full; the authority would not go out of existence.

2) The authority had power to build only two bridges and their approaches. Moses added additional wording that permitted the construction of "new roads, streets, parkways or avenues connecting with the approaches." The simple word "connecting" permitted Moses to build whatever he wanted so long as it eventually hooked up with the bridge.

3) Under the structure, the fiscal agent of the authority received and paid out the corporation's funds. To get around this, Moses buried another simple clause in his bill: "The money shall be paid out on checks of the comptroller on requisition of the Chairman of the Authority." With this change, only

Chairman Moses could spend money; the fiscal agent became his gofer.

4) To ensure that no legislative body could take away his power, Moses worked in the ultimate protection. Biographer Caro reports: "He did it in Section 9, Paragraph 2 and 4, Clauses a through i. Paragraph 2 authorized the authority to pass resolutions governing the sale of its bonds. The various clauses of Paragraph 4 said, when taken together, that the resolutions could contain provisions dealing with toll rules, Authority rules and regulations and *'any other matters, of like or different character, which in any way affect the security on the protection of the bonds.'* And Paragraph 4 also said that any such resolution "shall be a part of the contract with the holders of the bonds."

Since the U.S. Constitution forbids state or local governments to "pass any...legislation impairing the obligation of contracts," the tax-exempt bond covenants protected forever Moses' power base. No governor, mayor, legislator, not even public opinion could abrogate his power. In addition, he could now finance his dreams without relying on the whims of the state legislature.

For 40 years, Robert Moses maintained his power base. He outmaneuvered five governors and six mayors, and he defied and beat at the power game his greatest enemy, President Franklin D. Roosevelt. Even with all of this, his greatest legacy is that the nation followed his lead when he rewrote the rules of municipal finance. Self-perpetuating authorities that circumvent debt limitations, and the ballot box, are now commonplace. The largest issuing states now number the bond-issuing authorities within their borders not in the tens, but in the hundreds.

John N. Mitchell and the Moral Obligation Bond

Most people who remember John Mitchell remember him as the tough, poker-faced, pipe-smoking figure of the Watergate hearings. True, he befriended Richard Nixon, managed his successful 1968 presidential campaign, served as U.S. Attorney General, and was scorched by the Watergate scandal. But his legacy was his influence on municipal finance.

John N. Mitchell, born in Detroit in 1913, grew up on Long Island, N.Y. He played semi-pro hockey to pay his way through

Fordham University and its law school. He joined the municipal bond law firm of Caldwell and Raymond in 1938; by 1942 he was a partner.

During World War II, he served as a naval commander in the South Pacific, and was Ensign John F. Kennedy's commanding officer. After the war, he returned to Caldwell, and in 1966 the firm merged with a firm that became known as Nixon, Mudge, Rose, Guthrie, Alexander and Mitchell.

Mitchell was recognized as one of the most brilliant municipal bond attorneys. It was he who created the mechanism that permitted the State of Wisconsin to evade its archaic constitutional bond limitation of $250,000 of debt. And it was Mitchell, as counsel to New York's Gov. Nelson Rockefeller, who came up with the idea that permitted the governor to get around voter disapproval of his numerous bond schemes. The concept: the moral obligation bond..

When he took office in January 1959, Rockefeller had grandiose plans to rebuild housing in New York's inner cities. As a graduate of the Robert Moses school of issuing debt, he had the state legislature create the Housing Finance Agency — one of 230 authorities created during his 15-year tenure. John Mitchell was called in for an opinion by Commissioner of Housing James Gaynor. In Mitchell's judgment, the "Investment community was pretty sour on that type of obligation" and would demand a high rate of interest. To change the negative perception, he added language to the authority's indenture that included the "legislative intent" to supply money, in the event of revenue shortfalls, to meet principal and interest payments. Since the state had no legal obligation to aid the authority, the concept became known as a "moral obligation."

In a November 1984 interview with *The Bond Buyer*, Mitchell gave this perspective:

Q. How did the idea for the moral obligation bond come about?

A. [When] Nelson Rockefeller was elected the governor of New York in 1958, the voters turned down all of the propositions that had to be voted under the state constitution — for housing, mental health, etc. His director of housing was telling me about the state's problems.

In order to keep the interest cost down and have a security that would be marketable, I transferred over to the Housing

Finance Agency a concept [of moral obligation bonds] that had been used temporarily in connection with school districts.

I just took that and adapted it to the Housing Finance Agency and structured the mechanics of it. It went very, very well and the bonds were marketable, the interest rates were more than reasonable, and, of course, we took it from there.

Q. Critics of moral obligation bonds say they are a form of political elitism that bypasses the voter's right to a referendum or an initiative.

A. That's exactly the purpose of them.

The technique worked. The bond rating agencies accepted it, and the Office of the Comptroller of the Currency ruled that banks could buy and underwrite the bonds when it declared the debt was much the same as general obligation.

Over the years, Rockefeller expanded the state's moral obligation to finance the State University Construction Fund, nursing, nonprofit housing, and health facility and hospital programs. The Battery Park City Authority and the City University Dormitory Authority also managed to obtain the state's moral obligation.

In 1968, after the assassination of Martin Luther King, Rockefeller convinced the state legislature to approve the creation of the Urban Development Corporation. Backed with the state's moral obligation, the UDC's mandate was to build housing in "substandard, blighted areas." Poorly run, the investment community refused to underwrite additional debt and on Feb. 25, 1975, the agency defaulted on $104.5 million of notes. Eventually the state came up with the money and maintained the integrity of its moral obligation.

The UDC defaulted at the same time that New York City was running into fiscal difficulties. The events were unrelated. As Mitchell explained to *The Bond Buyer:*

Q. Some have argued that, by overextending the debt of various bond-issuing authorities, these bonds contributed to New York City's 1975 financial crisis, the city's high tax burden, declining population, and the flight of industry. Were these bonds really issued for the public good?

A. First of all, moral obligation bonds were designed to get around the [state] constitution so that you didn't require the referendum. Second, the use of moral obligations may very well have been overextended, which required the state's contributions. I don't believe you'll find that to be true in connection with the original concept set up with the Housing Finance Agency.

With respect to New York City, obviously what the state did through this moral obligation financing had nothing whatever to do with the city. The concept under which the financings were done was such that it was reasonably anticipated that the revenues that flowed from these projects would take care of the required debt service, or lease-rental payments, and consequently there would be no necessity for a call upon the state appropriations.

Unfortunately, they thought they had a very good thing going there, and they've extended it into fields where the revenues from the projects didn't meet the anticipated debt service requirements. That necessitated the state appropriations.

Tax-exempt moral obligation debt has endured, and today over 20 states have issued this kind of revenue bond. And in New York State, moral obligation debt, which stood at $844 million in 1969, now totals over $12 billion.

The Default of the Century: WPPSS

In August 1983, the Washington Public Power Supply System defaulted on interest payments due on $2.25 billion bonds. This was the single largest default in the history of municipal finance and the reverberations from the debacle are still being felt.

According to *The Bond Buyer's* Howard Gleckman, "the supply system fell victim to Murphy's Law. Everything that could go wrong did." To understand what happened, an examination of events going back over half a century is essential.

The Bonneville Power Administration was established by an Act of Congress in 1937. Its purpose was to sell excess hydroelectric power generated from federal dams built in the Pacific Northwest during the Depression and to construct and operate transmission facilities that transferred the power to public and private utilities.

As the Northwest began to grow, Bonneville found itself selling wholesale electric power to 146 utility, industrial and governmental customers that encompassed 300,000 square miles and eight million people. Unlike the Tennessee Valley

Authority, which had the ability to generate and market electrical power, BPA had a limited mandate: it could only sell power from existing dams. With increased power demands, it became evident that hydroelectricity, which could not be stored, would not provide enough power for the region.

Attempting to cope with this problem, in September 1956 17 public utility districts in the State of Washington sought permission to form an authority that would seek a regional takeover of federal dams. The ability to form this group was permitted under the 1930 Public Power Act, which established guidelines for creating public power authorities. In January 1957, the request was granted and the Washington Public Power Supply System was born.

Those running WPPSS quickly changed its reason for being: instead of purchasing existing federal projects, they would build their own power generating plants.

In 1960, WPPSS began construction on its first power project, the Packwood Lake Dam in Washington State. Financed with tax-exempt bonds yielding 2.6%, it was completed late and with a 25% cost overrun. Operations began in June 1964 under a cloud — various design faults came to light when a construction contractor brought a lawsuit against the system.

WPPSS continued to eye expansion, and in 1966, after much haggling with the U.S. Government, took over a federal plutonium plant. With a $60 million federal grant, it converted the plant into a power-producing installation. BPA, the power transmitter, kept a close eye on WPPSS; it did not want a repeat of the Packwood problems.

During the 1960s and 1970s, the Northwest experienced substantial growth, and the optimistic predictions of continued growth and the ensuing electrical power demands influenced the powers at BPA and WPPSS. They bought the prediction of the Pacific Northwest Utilities Conference Committee that power supplies would have to increase 7.5% annually. With these guesstimates in hand, BPA decided that hydro power alone was not enough. It turned to WPPSS to supply nuclear power to meet the anticipated needs.

Construction began on the first nuclear plant (named Project 2 since it was radically different from the first planned project at Hanford) in August 1971. It was to generate 1,100 megawatts, cost $397.5 million and be ready in September 1977. The building of the second plant (known as Project 1) was authorized in 1974 and was to be built in the vicinity of Project 2. This plant was to generate 1,250 megawatts and was to cost $632.9 million.

Finally, Project 3, to be built in Grays Harbor County, was approved to begin construction in July 1975. In order to secure the necessary financial support, this 1,240-megawatt plant (estimated costs: $581.4 million) was to be owned 70% by WPPSS and 30% by investor-owned utilities. To meet these ends, WPPSS expanded its membership to the cities of Richland, Seattle, Tacoma and Ellensburg in Washington, and also offered shares in the projects to Idaho, Oregon, Wyoming, Nevada and Montana.

In the minds of many, these three projects were still not enough to meet future needs. WPPSS announced plans for a fourth and fifth project; unlike the first three, though, BPA would not take part in the deals. The reader should note that the U.S. Department of Energy, acting through the BPA, agreed to purchase, if necessary, the entire electrical capability of Projects 1, 2 and 3 from investor-owned utility customers who purchased such power from WPPSS. Bonneville is thus obligated to pay the total annual costs of each so-called net billed project, including the debt service on the bonds, whether or not the project is completed or ever operating.

Although the BPA does not have the direct pledge of the federal government, it can increase customer rates to meet principal and interest payments. Since Projects 4 and 5 did not have BPA backing, they leaned on 88 utilities to guarantee the costs of the projects in the form of "take or pay contracts." The utilities, in effect, agreed to pay the entire costs of the projects and to purchase their entire electrical output whether or not the plants were ever completed or if the utilities needed the power.

The five projects were to cost $4.1 billion, but this figure jumped to $6.67 billion in 1976, $11.9 billion in 1979, and $23.8 billion in 1981. Tax-exempt bonds were being issued in $200 million clips every 90 days, and WPPSS became the number one issuer of bonds. Investors, particularly institutions, naturally reached a saturation point where they could not approve additional portfolio purchases of the bonds. By February 1982, in order to make a new deal palatable, WPPSS' investment bankers had to price the bonds at a 15.12% coupon rate.

As the cost overruns were hemorrhaging, it was realized that expected growth in energy demand would be more like 1.5% annually, not the projected 7.5%. There would be little need for Project 4 and 5 power; hence the provisions of the "take or pay" contracts were likely to be triggered.

Panic began to set in. Discussions to mothball Projects 4 and 5 began. Participants balked at the amount of money they would have to pay to implement the shutdown; citizens began to realize the potential increase in their electrical rates and boycotted local utilities and a bank that served as WPPSS' trustee.

In January 1982, Projects 4 and 5 were cancelled, and in April, construction of Project 1 was halted for up to five years. With these changes, the total estimated costs dropped from $23.8 billion to $8.2 billion.

In May, the trustee for Projects 4 and 5 bonds, Chemical Bank, asked a Washington State Court to order WPPSS and its participants to repay $2.25 billion in principal and nearly $5 billion in interest to bondholders. In September, an Oregon court declared that the contracts signed by its state's utilities were void. The court said that the participants overstepped their authority when they signed the agreements. The Washington court ruled in October that the state's take-or-pay contracts were legal, but that decision was overturned by the state's highest court in June 1983.

During these court battles, the 88 participants in Projects 4 and 5 were expected to pony up $190 million for the July 1, 1983, debt service payment. The funds did not materialize, and during May and June, the credit ratings on Projects 4 and 5 bonds were suspended. WPPSS admitted in July 1983 that it couldn't make the payments, and Chemical Bank, the trustee, forced default when it demanded the repayment of all the outstanding bonded debt on the two projects.

Many of the events that led to this disaster were beyond the control of WPPSS and its sponsors; but as *The Bond Buyer's* Howard Gleckman described, many were not: "Paid millions of dollars to raise money to build massive projects, Wall Street failed to do its job. It started what it could not finish. It let short-term greed overcome longer-range concerns. It ignored evidence that the projects might not be feasible. Later, its desperate effort to salvage the projects cost WPPSS and its investors billions more in wasted money. To many, the story of

WPPSS is as much the failure of Wall Street as it is of the supply system, Bonneville, and the region's utilities and contractors."

After the default, the stage was set for the biggest fraud trial ever. It began in September 1988, but eventually every one of the 160 defendants in the case settled. The 24,000 bondholders sued the utilities, engineers, bond counsel, rating agencies, underwriters and financial advisers. Some claims were dismissed. The remainder eventually settled for various amounts totaling a little less than 50 cents on the dollar of principal, and none of the more than $5 billion in interest that was owed.

In September 1989, WPPSS did what once seemed impossible — it returned to the municipal bond market to borrow more money .The agency succeeded in refunding nearly $3 billion in debt carrying coupons ranging from 9% to the mid-teens.

Assaults on Tax-Exemption

Tax-exempt bonds have been under steady fire since the creation of the federal income tax in 1913.

In mid-1918, for example, *The Daily Bond Buyer,* as it was then styled, carried a story on the House Ways and Means Committee's move to tax state and municipal bonds. The debate dragged on for months, until in October the newspaper reported that the Senate Finance Committee killed the so-called "municipal bond tax" because it thought the measure was unconstitutional. The newspaper noted at the time, "It is now generally believed that the controversy . . is ended. Surely, nothing further can be added to the strong case against such taxation that has been offered by numerous legal experts . . . and it would be improbable that any further attempt to legislate along these lines will be made. . . . "

Little did it know. In December 1920, Rep. McFadden of the House Banking and Currency Committee introduced a bill to remove tax-exemption. The *Detroit Free Press,* in an editorial in 1921 entitled "The Tax-Exempt Bond Evil, " said , "The tax-exempt bond has become a serious problem in America," and urged its abolition. President Warren G. Harding jumped on the tax-exempt abolition bandwagon. But *The New York Times* editorialized, "The President errs, he treats the symptom instead of the disease, when he suggests a Constitutional amendment to do away with tax-exempt securities. The evil, as he sees it, is that taxpayers invest in these securities, and so escape the levy. The truth is that just and equitable taxation is not evaded. When men in large numbers seek out ways to escape their taxes, it is axiomatic that the fault is with the taxes; they are taxes such as never ought to be laid. If the surtaxes were reduced to a decent, civilized level, if the futile, senseless passion for punishing the rich could be cudgeled out of the heads of the heads of the Grangers and Populists in Congress, there would be no trouble about the tax-exempt securities." The move went down to defeat. ·

Until, that is, 1933, when House leaders killed what *The Daily Bond Buyer* termed a "very objectionable provision" against tax-exemption, originally sponsored by Sen. Cordell Hull. It was buried. But that only marked the beginning of what would be a long assault on tax-exempts throughout the life of the New Deal.

In 1934, 1935, and again in 1938 and 1939, New Dealers attacked tax-exemption. In January 1941, *The Daily Bond Buyer* wrote in its weekly "Washington Letter" column: "Associations of States and municipalities apparently will again be faced with a solid front of Federal authorities when the issue is again brought before Congress."

On Jan. 20, Secretary of the Treasury Henry Morgenthau called for the elimination of "the inequitable tax-exemption on interest from governmental securities." Morgenthau noted that "every administration for the past 20 years has recommended the complete elimination of tax-exempt securities." In March, the Treasury decided to "force the issue" by taxing income from the Port Authority of New York and New Jersey's bond issues, in what would become known as the Shamberg case, so-called because Alexander J. Shamberg, a commissioner of the Port Authority, was one of the bondholders sued.

In 1942, President Roosevelt asked for the abolition of tax-exemption, as did Mariner Eccles, chairman of the Federal Reserve Board, and Secretary Morgenthau, who even toyed for a time with the idea of taxing all outstanding issues. The nation's governors, mayors and treasurers rallied to lobby Congress against the proposal. Morgenthau stuck by his guns, and Roosevelt later threatened to introduce a kind of alternative minimum tax on incomes over $25,000.

The battle raged throughout 1943. In January 1944, the U.S. Tax Court ruled in the Shamberg case, upholding the tax-exemption of the Port Authority. At the time, *The Daily Bond Buyer* noted, "A decision upholding the express exemption of the Authorities under the language of the Revenue Act precludes any reconsideration by the Court of the continuing validity of the doctrine of *Pollock v. Farmers Loan and Trust Co.,* the case which since 1896 has stood as a constitutional barrier to federal taxation of state and local municipal bonds."

The U.S. Supreme Court refused to review the decision of the U.S. Tax Court. In January 1945, the newspaper wrote, "No Treasury official in high position will say for quotation what the next move will be toward winning the long (and sometimes bitter) contest to tax state and municipal bond income. But there is no indication that the refusal of the Supreme Court to review the decisions of the United States Tax Court . . . ends the matter."

The Bond Buyer editorialized, "The Treasury finds itself right back where it started. It now remains to be seen whether officials of that Department will admit that the proper approach to this problem is the submission to the States of a carefully drawn constitutional amendment which, while preserving the doctrine of reciprocal immunity between the Federal and the State governments, would permit each to tax income derived from each other's securities. The only alternative is to renew efforts, which have repeatedly met with defeat, to induce Congress to authorize the Treasury to assess the income tax on municipal bond interest and thus put the question of power to tax such interest once more up to the Supreme Court."

In 1951, the Treasury again asked for an end to tax-exemption. It was beaten back. In 1967, the Treasury ruled that industrial development bonds were no longer tax-exempt, but in 1968 Congress overruled the Treasury's action with the passage of the Revenue and Expenditure Control Act, which exempted certain kinds of IDBs from taxation.

It was not until the 1980s that tax-exemption was seriously attacked again. Fresh from an historic landslide that reaffirmed his 1980 mandate, President Ronald Reagan introduced on May 28, 1985, a tax-reform plan that would drop income tax rates to eliminate most loopholes and simplify the tax code.

The South's $300 Million Repudiation
Civil War-era bonds declared invalid:

Alabama	$812,000
Arkansas	$20,807,000
Florida	$5,280,000
Georgia	$13,580,000
Louisiana	$32,115,000
Mississippi	$22,600,000
North Carolina	$48,350,000
South Carolina	$19,500,000
Tennessee	$29,850,000
Virginia	$72,220,000

Source: The Bond Buyer, May 13, 1904.

Municipal Bond Defaults by Number of Issues 1940-1988

Period	Number of defaulted issues	Total number of issues	Default rate
1940-49	79	40,907	0.2%
1950-59	112	74,592	0.2
1960-69	294	79,941	0.4
1970-83	200	118,063	0.2
1984-88	508	46,268	1.1
Total	**1,193**	**359,771**	**0.3%**

Source: Public Securities Association

The history of what became the Tax Reform Act of 1986 actually began in 1983, when Sen. Bill Bradley and Rep. Richard Gephardt, both Democrats, introduced their own version of tax reform. A similar plan was later introduced by Republican Sen. William Roth and Rep. Jack Kemp. In November 1984, the Treasury introduced its own plan, a dramatic proposal that would have wound up cutting the tax-exempt market by two-thirds.

The various components of tax reform were considered by Congress for more than a year, and the battle was accompanied by all sorts of scares and shocks to the market, perhaps the nastiest of all coming on March 19, 1986, when Sen. Bob Packwood, chairman of the Senate Finance Committee, proposed a tax on all municipal bonds, and the tax-exempt market shut down trading for the day.

It was not until April 29, 1986, that the package picked up steam. Sen. Packwood put together a plan that included a top individual tax rate of 27%. On May 7, the Senate Finance Committee approved the plan 20-0. With momentum building, the tax reform debate began on June 4 and the bill was passed 97-3 on June 24. The House of Representatives, which passed its own version in December, now joined the Senate in conference to hammer away differences. By Sept. 27, the House and Senate approved the Conference Report compromises and the bill was sent to the White House. On Oct. 22, 1986, with much fanfare, President Reagan signed the bill into law.

The legislation had a dramatic impact on the municipal bond industry. Years after its effective date, the industry is still trying to recover from its implications.

The chief objections of the tax writers in Congress were bonds benefiting private activities, particularly industrial development bonds. IDBs were born in the Depression, were ruled taxable in 1967, and returned to tax-exempt status in 1968. By 1982, IDB volume shot up to around $44 billion, more than half of the $77 billion in tax-exempt debt sold, and they were being used by states to finance everything from factories and industrial parks to sports facilities and motels. The Tax Reform Act of 1986 put the lid on such financings, literally capping how much each state could sell in such bonds.

The act not only did away with some kinds of bonds and curbed others, but also managed to divide the tax-exempt market into tiers. In particular, it created the "bank-qualified bond," sold by municipalities that reasonably expect to sell less than $10 million of tax-exempt bonds a year. They are the only bonds for which commercial banks can still deduct 80% of the interest they incur to carry municipal bond inventories. With the original deduction gone, so was banks' interest in holding on to large positions.

Tax reform also created "alternative minimum tax" bonds, tax-exempt bonds that are in fact subject to tax when held by certain individuals and corporations.

The upshot of tax reform was a structural change in the market: not only what kinds of bonds were issued, but also who would buy them. The market went from one in which property and casualty insurance companies and other institutional investors predominated to one led by retail buyers. And retail investors, more often than not, do not actively trade their bonds but hold them until maturity.

The Aftermath of Tax Reform

These tax reform restrictions took their toll, and 1987 was labelled by bond industry wags as "the year to forget." *The Bond Buyer* reported in December of that year, "The tax-exempt market faced the hardest transition of all the credit markets. It had to cope with declining volume brought about by the Tax Reform Act (under $100 billion, down from over $142.54 billion in 1986 and a record $203.95 billion in 1985), narrowing underwriting fees, and the loss of some of the biggest players in the market."

In addition to these adjustments, a volatile market which led to estimated trading losses of $500 million in April and May caused many firms to begin reassessing their commitment to the tax-exempt market. The major shock to the industry was when Salomon Brothers Inc., which had been the top underwriter in the nation, decided on Oct. 12, 1987, to close its municipal bond department.

The abrupt dismissal of over 200 bond professionals from Salomon marked the end of the municipal market's "Golden Age." The stock market crash and the staggering losses it dealt to firms a week later only served to steel those firms resolve to wade in and cut or entirely eliminate departments that had long outlived the municipal market's 1980 to 1985 boom.

"Firms who didn't see it all happening in 1986 must have had their heads in the sand, or someplace else," said Austin V. Koenen, then a managing director of public finance at Shearson Lehman Hutton Inc. and chairman of the Public Securities Association's municipal securities division.

"What happened was, people got fat, dumb, and happy, and income expectations outstripped reasonable expectations. Tax reform was meant to cut volume, and guess what? It did. If there's less volume, there will be more competition, and if there's more competition, spreads will go down. Is anybody really surprised?" he said.

The bloodletting also made the contrasts between doing business in New York and doing business everywhere else starker than ever. Small and regional bond dealers for the most part never built up the massive overhead New York investment banks did by "hiring legions of MBAs specializing in all kinds of esoteric financings," one Midwestern banker said.

Other events did not help morale in the municipal bond industry. On April 20, 1989, the Supreme Court ruled that municipal bonds were not guaranteed tax-exempt status by the Constitution. On Sept. 22, the Securities and Exchange Commission released its long awaited and critical report on the $2.25 billion WPPSS default. On the same day, the SEC also released a report stating that underwriters had an obligation to account for the accuracy of official statements before they bid, or sign off, on deals. Those with a perverse sense of logic can skip right to Chapter 9, "The Regulators," for a look at the municipal bond market today.

Chapter 2:

General Obligation Bonds and Notes: What Are They? How Are They Analyzed?

The history and growth of municipal finance and the function served by the general obligation bond are shining examples of federalism and the orderly response of local government to the needs and desires of its citizenry.

This chapter will give an overview of the creation of local governmental entities and an examination of the development and role of the financial instrument known as the general obligation bond.

To ensure an understanding of local government and its ability to raise capital necessary to finance various projects, there will be an examination of the State of New York, its political subdivisions, and their constitutional prerogatives. An official statement for the bond sale of one New York municipality, the city of Rochester, will be reviewed. The same method will also be used to analyze a City of Chicago credit. These critiques should provide the reader with the basics to analyze a municipal credit and to grasp the relationship between government and its economic and political demographics when raising capital to provide services.

The Debut of the General Obligation Bond

The GO bond is the oldest and most basic form of municipal finance in the U.S. As American cities began to grow in the early 19th century, raising revenues for schools, roads and waterworks by the traditional means of public land sales, donations, lotteries and current taxation became impractical. To build a project rapidly and to avoid exhausting the taxpayer, it was essential to incur debt whose repayment could be spread over a long period of time. Hence, the birth of the general improvement bond.

Most historians of public finance agree that New York City issued the first bonds as early as 1812. The concept was adopted throughout the nation, and between 1820 and 1840 most of America's major cities experimented with municipal bonds.

Special assessment and special district obligation bonds began to appear during this period. They generally financed railroads, canals and irrigation projects. Many of these programs were short-lived due to the depression that hit the country in 1837. Reacting to numerous defaults, state legislatures amended their constitutions to limit the many fly-by-night special districts. The "pay as you go" concept was popularized to prohibit the abuse and to retard the exhausting of the local tax base.

Until the first World War, the general improvement bond supplied the bulk of the capital to meet the needs of the community. These bonds were structured with the principal and interest owed to the creditor guaranteed by the "full faith and credit" of the municipality. All the taxable real estate within the municipality was subject to the levy of ad valorem taxes (property taxes) to pay the bonds and interest without limitation as to rate or amount.

The Property Tax

Historically, the general property tax has been despised. In the U.S., "wealth" was measured by real property (land and buildings). Voting rights were often based on property ownership; hence it was deemed equitable that those who approved bond issues at the polls pay for those decisions. By 1932, 97% of all local revenues were derived from the property tax.

When an individual buys a house, there is the real value (the purchase price) and the assessed value (for the purpose of levying property taxes) determined by the local municipality. Discrepancies in neighborhood evaluations occur frequently because of the human factor—the assessor. "Rule of thumb" is often used to estimate assessed value. Also, inflation and the inability to reassess houses on a regular basis contributes to the lopsidedness of evaluations even on the same block.

The total assessed value of a municipality is the tax base. The tax rate is then determined according to the amount of money required to meet principal and interest payments for the fiscal year. If one assumes a $1 billion tax base and $15 million needed for principal and interest payments: $15 million divided by $1 billion equals .015, or 1.5%. So, the tax rate would be 1.5% of the assessed valuation of an individual's home. If one assumes assessed home value of $250,000, multiply 1.5% by $250,000 to get $3,750 in yearly property taxes.

There are those who argue that the property tax is inequitable. They suggest that political sub-divisions have different exemptions and different emphasis on programs that discriminate against poorer districts. Although the U.S. Supreme Court has upheld the principle that different educational standards, objectives and costs implemented by wealthier school districts do not violate the Constitution's equal protection clause, state courts are rejecting this view.

On Oct. 2, 1989, the Texas Supreme Court unanimously ruled that the state's financial formula for education was unconstitutional due to "glaring disparities" between rich and poor school districts. In New Jersey, that state's highest court ruled in June 1990: "We find that under the present system the evidence compels but one conclusion: the poorer the district and the greater its need, the less the money available, and the worse the education.. . . . We hold that the Act must be amended to assure funding of education in poorer urban districts at the level of property-rich districts; that such funding cannot be allowed to depend on the ability of local school districts to tax; that such funding must be guaranteed and mandated by the State."

New Jersey must now make sure that poor districts spend the same amount as wealthy districts. If a rich district's citizens choose by way of ballot box to increase their education budget, the state, to maintain equality, must automatically increase aid to the poorer areas. This requirement encouraged Gov. James Florio to cut local aid to many districts in order to shift the dollars to poorer districts. The result was that already heavily taxed districts were forced to increase property taxes even higher to meet shortfalls.

Property Tax Revolts

In recent years there have been citizen property tax revolts, most notably in California, where in 1978 voters passed Proposition 13, an initiative limiting ad valorem property taxes to 1% of market value and annual increases in tax bills to no more than 2%; and in Massachusetts, where voters in 1981 voted to limit property tax levels in the state to 2 1/2% of assessed valuation.

In both cases, issuance of local general obligation debt was cut fairly dramatically, at least until local officials and investment bankers concocted such things as Mello-Roos financing and various other flexible ways to pay for services. As James Ring Adams wrote in his book, *Secrets of the Tax Revolt* (1984), "Public debt is the Achilles heel of all attempts to limit government spending and taxing....The framers of Proposition

13 and of all tax initiatives have to choose between clamping down on debt, risking deterioration of infrastructure, or treating it flexibly, risking widespread evasion of fiscal controls."

In recent years, a number of major tax limitation initiatives in various states have been defeated at the polls, suggesting that the citizenry, for the time being, is more willing to foot the bill for local goods and services. Indeed, in the presidential election of 1988, voters also approved a record $15 billion in new municipal bonding authority.

The Role of Local Government: Growing Responsibilities

During the past 60 years, the American people, tempered by the Depression and three wars, changed their perception regarding the role of local government. At the turn of the century, cities, towns and villages furnished the basics: schools, roads and police protection. Today, local government has become one of the largest "businesses" in the U.S. economy. The states and their political subdivisions spend over $700 billion a year and employ over 10 million people. Local government is now responsible for water, sewers, mass transportation, gas and electricity, industrial aid, pollution control, hospitals and housing.

In 1925, the total volume of new municipal debt stood at $1.4 billion. By 1989, that figure had reached more than $700 billion, comprised of such esoteric financing vehicles as tax-exempt commercial paper, put option bonds, variable rate securities, zero coupon bonds, warrants and municipal leases.

Additional pressure on state and local governments to increase their responsibilities have come from Washington, D.C., with the federal government mandating that local governments provide various services or conform to specified procedures. The Environmental Protection Agency, for example, has ordered municipalities to implement uniform clean water standards. This federally unfunded program has forced many political subdivisions to pay for federal mandates and cut back on other kinds of financings.

But the government has also put pressure on municipalities to increase their activities by providing chunks of money, called grants-in-aid, in order for them to tackle certain projects. But the government entity that accepts the funds must raise the remaining dollars.

In the early part of the century, grants-in-aid programs were geared toward the rural poor. By the 1960s, the vast majority of the grants concentrated on urban areas. The controversial Maternity Aid Grant program, created in 1921, established the supremacy of congressional discretion concerning these projects. The Commonwealth of Massachusetts not only rejected participation in the Maternity Aid Act, it also challenged the constitutionality of the program. Since the state was not coerced to participate, the court upheld congressional legislative action to disperse funds as it saw fit, and ruled that Massachusetts had no grounds to sue.

New York State Municipalities and How They Can Incur Debt

The State of New York has led the nation in providing services to its populace by means of innovative financings. New York's vast urban population, its wealth and its power structure have permitted the creative genius of a Robert Moses and a strong chief executive like Nelson Rockefeller to flourish.

There are over 2,300 political subdivisions in New York, and many of the agencies and authorities that were implemented by the state government are looked upon as models for the rest of the nation to emulate. As described in Chapter One, many of the concepts led to abuses that culminated in the 1975 financial crisis. Nevertheless, the boldness and genius involved cannot be denied.

The Constitution of the State of New York deals extensively with the ability of the government to incur bonded debt. Article 7 describes the debt that can be contracted by the state; Article 8 labels the debt permitted by local governments; Article 18 deals with public housing debt. And the state legislature, in compliance with the constitution, has created state and local finance laws that limit governments from abusing their ability to incur debt and from overburdening the local tax base.

The people of New York are protected by the constitution because the amount of debt burden that can be permitted must be approved at the ballot box. They have the right to reject state bond issues as well as local school district projects.

On the   state level, some exceptions to voter approval are permitted:

1. Short -term tax and revenue anticipation notes.

2. Debt required to repel invasion, revolt or war.

3. Debt required to suppress forest fires.

The constitution specifically permits the following debt:

1. $300 million may be incurred for the elimination of railroad crossings. (Article 7, Section 14)

2. $250 million of debt is allowed for the expansion of the State University system. (Article 7, Section 19)

3. $300 million may be contracted for urban renewal. These housing bonds are to be dedicated to providing low rent housing. (Article 18, Section 3)

Tax anticipation and revenue anticipation notes that are issued by the state must be liquidated within one year. Bond anticipation notes must be rolled into long-term bonds within two years. All bonded state debt must be paid for in equal annual installments and a given issue cannot have a life beyond 40 years. In addition, the debt of any given project cannot exceed the expected life or purpose of the undertaking.

The revenues needed to pay yearly principal and interest must be approved by the legislature and segregated by the comptroller. The constitution provides the essential safeguard against legislative tinkering: "If at any time the Legislature shall fail to make any such appropriation, the Comptroller shall set apart from the first revenues thereafter received applicable to the General Fund of the State, a sum sufficient to pay such interest and installments of principal, and shall so apply the monies thus set apart. In such circumstances, the Comptroller may be required to set aside and apply such revenues as aforesaid, at the suit of any holder of such bonds " (Article 7, Section 16).

Local municipalities (counties, cities, towns and villages) come under similar constitutional restraints as the state. But all local debt must be secured by the full faith and credit of the political subdivision. This generally means the local property tax. To ensure that localities do not abuse the privilege and overburden the individual taxpayer, the framers of the state constitution listed specific tax limitations, many in effect to this day. The following curbs are based on the percentage of the average full valuation of taxable real estate. (The average consists of the current year and four prior years.)

Debt Limits:
- Nassau County , 10%;
- any county other than Nassau County , 7%;
- New York City , 10%;
- any city, other than New York City, having 125,000 or more inhabitants, 9%;
- any city having less than 125,000 inhabitants, excluding education purposes, 7%;
- any town or village, 7%;
- any school district which is coterminous with, or partly within or wholly within, a city having less than 125,000 inhabitants for education purposes, 5%; provided however, that such limitation may be increased in relation to indebtedness for specified objects or purposes with 1) the approving vote of 60% or more of the duly qualified voters of such school district voting on a proposition therefor submitted at a general or special election 2) the consent of the Regents of the University of the State of New York and 3) the consent of the state comptroller.

The constitution does permit certain exclusions from debt computation, including debt for water supply, self-supporting debt, and tax and revenue anticipation notes.

New York's general obligation debt is, thus, iron-clad in its full faith and credit backing. But, as author Adams noted in *Secrets of the Tax Revolt,* "state finance in general, and New York's in particular, has been marked by the ballooning of special kinds of debt insulated from . . . voter control. These limited liability issues carry the backing mainly of the special-district or 'public-benefit' authority that produced them. These arrangements, sometimes supplemented by special devices like 'lease-purchase' deals, have allowed state and local governments to incur better than $20 billion of debt a year without the approval or even the scrutiny of the taxpayer....The history of New York shows that apparently definitive constitutional language can be evaded on a massive scale."

The New York legislature in 1990 briefly considered a comprehensive measure proposed by Gov. Mario Cuomo to re-form municipal finance, and it is likely to do so again. The measure would in general have allowed local governments more flexibility in structuring their bond sales and debt ser-vice, as well as raised the maximum amount of bonds that can be sold by localities through negotiation, now capped at

$500,000. The legislature finally passed a bill allowing localities to give 48 hours notice before entering the market with a competitive bond sale. Such shelf registration is common in the corporate bond market, but relatively new in the tax-exempt market. Yet it seems likely that the more comprehensive bill will be visited again in the future.

Rochester — Analyzing a General Obligation Bond Issue

With an understanding of the authority granted to New York municipalities to incur debt, it is now possible to examine a recent offering. This section will review and analyze the pertinent parts of an official statement for the city of Rochester. Rated A1 by Moody's, Rochester is located in western New York's Monroe County

The $20.5 million GO issue was dated Aug. 1, 1988. The issue consisted of serial bonds due Aug. 1, 1989, through 2002.

A review of portions of the official statement will give the reader an opportunity to understand the questions raised by the rating agencies and underwriters when determining the creditworthiness of a governmental entity.

Municipal analysis is not a science. When studying the demographics of a community, its debt ratios, general fund liquidity, tax burden, population and economic factors are reviewed. Based on the determinants of quality, the analyst must then make a value judgment as to whether or not the issuer has the ability to pay principal and interest on its outstanding bonded debt.

Purpose of the Issue

The proceeds from the sale of the Bonds will be applied to redeem $20,515,000 principal amount of outstanding bond anticipation notes of the City. The general categories of projects financed by the proceeds of such notes which are to be redeemed by the issuance of the bonds are:

Purpose	Amount
Construction, reconstruction, and improvement of schools	$5,000,000
Construction and reconstruction of City water supply system	$4,760,000
Construction and reconstruction of sewerage system	$2,620,000
Parking garages	$290,000
General Improvements	$7,845,000

Explanation: Money received from the issuance of the bonds will be used to retire outstanding bond anticipation notes. The New York State Constitution permits Bans to be rolled over twice before the municipality is required to issue long-term debt. In this case the proceeds are being used to finance typical improvements in a municipality.

Security for the Bonds

The Bonds are general obligations of the City for the payment of which the full faith and credit of the City will be pledged. The City has the power under the Constitution of the State by statute, and pursuant to the Bonds, the City will be obligated to levy on all taxable real property in the City such ad valorem taxes, without limitation as to rate or amount, as may be necessary to pay the principal of and interest on the Bonds. See "Certain Remedies of Bondholders on Default" and "Special Factors Affecting the Redemption and Marketability of the Bonds."

Explanation: The city has pledged its taxing power to pay principal and interest on its debt. If necessary, all revenues coming into the municipality will go to bondholders before any other goods or services are paid in full.

Certain Remedies of Bondholders

Under default in payment in full of the principal or interest on the Bonds, a holder of such defaulted Bonds has a contractual right to sue the City for the amount then due thereon. Such holder may obtain a judgment against the City with interest at the rate of nine percent per annum from the date of default in such payment or the date of demand therefore, if later. Execution or attachment of the City property probably cannot be obtained to satisfy the judgment. The General Municipal Law of the State provides that if the City fails to pay a final judgment for such principal and/or interest, it shall be the duty of the City Council to assess, levy and cause to be collected at the same time and in like manner as other moneys for expenses are then next thereafter to be assessed, levied and collected, a sum of money sufficient to pay said judgment with interest thereon and necessary fees and expenses. Any money so collected shall, from time to time, be paid to the judgment creditors.

The City Charter provides that upon final judgment against the City, the Corporation Counsel shall notify the City Council and the amount of such judgment must be raised in the next levy of taxes. Such judgment must be paid out of the first moneys paid into the City treasury on account of such levy. The City may also pay such judgment from available funds not otherwise appropriated. However, the rights of the judgment creditor are subject to stay and other laws affecting creditors' rights.

In addition, the State Constitution provides that if the City fails to provide in its annual budget, an amount sufficient to meet payment of principal of or interest on the Bonds, the City shall set aside from the first revenues thereafter received, an amount necessary to pay such amounts which were required to be included in the City's annual budget. In addition, the Director of Finance may be required to set apart and apply such revenues to the payment of and interest on the Bonds at the suit of any holder of the Bonds. Again, however, such right may be abridged by laws affecting creditors' rights or by laws involving financial emergencies.

The State Finance Law states that upon default in the payment of principal of, and/or interest on Bonds issued to finance school purposes, the State Comptroller is required to withhold, under certain conditions prescribed by State Finance Law, Section 99-b, State aid and assistance to the City, and to apply the amount thereof so withheld to the payment of such default principal and/or interest.

Explanation: This section spells out the bondholders' rights in the event of a default. The municipality can be forced by the creditor to levy the necessary taxes and to segregate that revenue to pay principal and interest. In addition, the issuer must pay a 9% penalty for the period the bonds are in default. It should be noted that the bondholder's rights are protected by the State Constitution, State Finance Law and the City of Rochester's charter.

State and Public Agency Fiscal Problems

The market for obligations of municipal issuers in New York may be affected by financial difficulties experienced by the State, certain of its agencies and certain political subdivisions in the State, including The City of New York, and any of such difficulties could affect general market conditions and the ability of the City to sell further obligations or, perhaps, to receive anticipated State aid payments.

The City is substantially dependent on financial assistance from the State, principally for aid to education, urban renewal aid, and general operating aid. In the 1987-88 City and School District Budgets, approximately 32.8% of the operating revenues of the City and School District Budgets are estimated to be received from the State as State aid. In the 1988-89 City and School District budgets, approximately 33% of the operating revenues of the City and School District Budgets are estimated to be received from the State as State aid. The State's budget for its fiscal year beginning April 1, 1988, has been adopted, and includes portions of such financial assistance to the City and its School District. The balance of such estimated State assistance is expected to be included in the State budget or its fiscal year beginning April 1, 1988.

Explanation: When analyzing a municipality, it is important to understand the extent of the political subdivision's dependence on inter-governmental aid. If a state is considered a declining credit because of its inability to balance its budget, the rating agencies may fear cutbacks in local aid. Such cutbacks could impair a municipality's creditworthiness and its ratings could be lowered.

In New York, localities are very dependent on state aid for education. With 33% of its education revenues dependent on the state budget, Rochester is below the average for municipalities in New York State.

Certain Limitations on the Taxing Power of the City

The New York State Constitution restricts the annual real property tax levy for operating expenses of two percent of average full value of taxable City property over the last five years. This limitation does not apply to taxes for debt service on the Notes.

Explanation: The State Constitution restricts the use of property tax revenues for the day-to-day operating expenses of the city. It does not apply to debt service on the bonds.

Economic Indicators

The economic vitality of a municipality is the most important factor when determining its future fiscal viability. One must examine the economic diversity, employment growth, residential and commercial building, and unemployment statistics during economic cycles.

A municipality could be headed for trouble if:

1. Building permits are growing at a slow pace or are declining.

2. Total population is declining, or a large percentage is elderly.

3. Total income is declining.

4. It is a one-industry town, or if wide cyclical variations in employment occur.

5. Retail sales are declining.

Population

Year	New York State	Rochester MSA	Monroe County	Rochester City
1970	18,241,391	961,516	711,917	294,977
1980	17,558,072	971,230	702,238	241,741
1982	17,659,000	995,900	707,400	244,094
1984	17,735,214	989,021	711,151	242,562
1985	17,966,200	1,001,100	713,200	243,000
1986	17,979,600	992,600	708,800	241,500

Population by Age: City of Rochester

Category	Number of Persons by Year		Percent of Total Population	
	1970	1980	1970	1980
0-18	95,941	68,772	32	28
19-34	73,130	76,374	25	32
35-64	86,770	62,784	29	26
65-plus	40,392	33,811	14	14
	296,233	**241,741**	**100**	**100**

Population trends are important in determining the desirability of a municipality as a place to live and work. Also, the age breakdown of the population can determine the types and expense of services the government must provide. A rapidly aging population can indicate increased demand for lower property taxes and less emphasis on education for the young. Such a political environment could discourage families of child-rearing age to emigrate to the area.

In the case of Rochester, the population has been stable for the past decade. At 14%, its senior citizen population does not dominate the area.

Unemployment Trends

Annual Average Unemployment—Monroe County and U.S.

1978	1979	1980	1981	1982	1983	1984	1985	1986	1987
Monroe County									
5.3	4.7	5.4	5.2	6.4	7.9	5.2	4.4	5.0	3.9%
U.S.									
6.0	5.8	7.1	7.6	9.7	9.6	7.5	6.7	7.0	6.2%

Unemployment data should be analyzed in relation to the nation as a whole. The nature of the municipality's unemployment during a national recession can give the analyst some indication of the extent that governmental revenues will suffer.

The Rochester area's unemployment has consistently been below the national average. Even at the height of the recession in 1982, Rochester's average unemployment was 34% below the national average.

Largest Employers

Number of

Rank/CompanyMajor Product Employees

1.	Eastman Kodak	Photographic equipment	45,530
2.	Xerox	Copying equipment	12,308
3.	Wegman's	Grocery	7,650
4.	University of Rochester	Education	5,378
5.	General Motors	Automotive Parts	5,190
6.	General Motors/Delco	Electronic Motors	3,895
7.	Bausch & Lomb	Vision Care Products	3,000
8.	Strong Memorial Hospital	Health Care	2,994
9.	Rochester General Hospital	Health Care	2,913
10.	Rochester Gas & Electric	Utility	2,575

Every analyst is leery of a municipality whose primary employment base is one company or industry. During periods of economic hardship, that major employer can cripple a town if it must resort to major layoffs or plant closings.

Areas that depend on automobile, textile or steel manufacturing are very susceptible to major unemployment peaks.

Although Eastman Kodak has for decades been an important employer in Rochester, numerous other nationally recognized corporations add to economic diversity.

Construction Activity

Number of Construction Permits Issued

	1983-84	1984-85	1985-86	1986-87	1987-88
New Residential	63	106	105	147	153
New Nonresidential	147	308	167	141	151
Residential Remodeling	631	472	760	790	741
Commercial Remodeling	587	421	669	651	678
Demolition	182	190	162	153	165
Conversions	337	372	132	78	66
Other structural	601	513	611	549	550
Plumbing	2,164	2,381	2,293	1,672	1,639
	4,712	4,763	4,899	4,181	4,143

The number of building permits issued by a municipality reflects the confidence of economic investors in the future of an area. Construction permits in Rochester have been relatively stable throughout the decade.

Comparative Review of Revenues and Expenditures

When reviewing the finances of a municipality, one's primary concerns should be the sources of taxes and the revenue trends. If income from taxes is limited to property taxes, this could result in a harsh burden on the owners of real estate. On the other hand, income from a sales tax can certainly ease the load. One must also note the trends in income and expenditures.

The following questions are frequently asked by analysts when reviewing a municipality's operating funds:

1. Has tax revenue increased yearly?
2. Are tax sources diversified?
3. Has intergovernmental aid increased?
4. Has the dependency on interfund transfers declined?
5. Has the growth of total revenues outpaced expenditures?
6. Has there been a cumulative deficit?
7. Has the growth of expenditures been constant with inflation? Rochester has consistently run small surpluses over the last few years. The proposed 1989 budget expects a modest increase in expenditures of only 2.6%. Also, there is to be no increase in the tax rate. The financial operations are satisfactory.

Debt Burden

Bonded Debt	Bans	TOTAL
$130,685,000	$26,394,250	$157,079,250

Debt Limitation of Rochester: $394,658,431
(Based on 9% of 5 year average full evaluation)
Maturities of Bonded Indebtedness
to be outstanding in 10 years: $4,055,000
Per Capita Direct Debt: $65
Per Capita Direct plus Overlapping Debt: $93
Direct Debt as a percentage of full valuation: 3.3%
Debt Service as a percentage of total expenditures: 4.9%

The basic questions one must consider when evaluating municipalities debt burden are:

1. Is per capita debt between $100 and $800?

2. Is total debt as a percentage of full valuation of real estate below 8%?

3. Is debt service as a percentage of total expenditures less than 8%?

4. Is the direct debt less than 50% of constitutional limits?

5. Will 50% of all debt be returned during the next 10 years?

In this case, Rochester appears to have a very light debt burden. Total debt per capita is very low at $93. Debt service as a percentage of expenditures stands at 4.9%, well below the 8% guideline. Over 90% of Rochester's debt will be repaid within 10 years, and the city has utilized only 39.8% of its bonded authority.

By applying the rules of thumb in analyzing a municipality's debt burden, it should be obvious why Rochester maintains its rating.

Examining Another GO Credit: The City of Chicago

Like most major urban centers, Chicago has had to contend with a declining and changing population, an increasing underclass, and an ancient infrastructure. Described by many pundits as the last of the big city machines, Chicago also has a colorful political history. From the 1932 assassination of the founder of the machine, Mayor Anton Cerniak, to the 20-year reign of Mayor Richard J. Daley; from the stormy administrations of Jane Byrne and Harold Washington to the reclaiming of the crown by Mayor Richard M. Daley, Chicago pols have dispensed thousands of jobs and contracts and millions of dollars.

By the mid-1980s, years of political infighting and machine excesses took their toll on the city's finances, and Moody's cut the city's GO rating to Baa. Running on a platform pledged to streamlining city government and balancing the budget, Harold Washington was elected the city's first black mayor. In the Jan. 18, 1988 ,issue of *Credit Markets,* Christopher O'Dea described Washington's efforts to secure an A rating:

"Mr. Washington's efforts won an award from the U.S. Conference of Mayors in February and in June, Standard & Poor's Corp. raised its ratings of the city's GO debt to A-minus from BBB-plus. Moody's Investors Service in October raised the city's rating to A from Baa1, reversing its March 1984 downgrade.

"The ratings upgrade culminated nearly five years of work to balance the city budget, improve financial data reporting and management, and set the city on a path toward a stable fiscal future. This was no small feat in a city that earned the nickname 'Beirut on the Lake' because of bitter fighting between the mayor and the city council."

Purpose of the Issue

The $53.8 million issue we will analyze below will be used to refund the city's Series 1987E bonds. Because the actual refunding of the bonds cannot take place until the July 1, 1997, call date, the proceeds of the issue (less the costs of issuance) will be invested in United States Treasury Obligations. The First National Bank of Chicago will be the trustee overseeing the investments.

Type of Bonds Issued

CLASS Bonds
Aggregate Original Principal Amount: $15,606,193.60

Denominations: In such amounts as will result in the total amount of principal and interest payable at maturity ("Compound Accreted Value at maturity") being equal to $5,000 or any integral multiple thereof.

Interest Payments: Interest will be paid only at maturity. Interest will be compounded semiannually on January 1 and July 1 of each of year, commencing July 1, 1991.

Maturity: January 1 in the years 2005 through 2012, inclusive.

Redemption: Not subject to redemption prior to maturity.

Education Grant: Each CLASS Bond representing $5,000 Compound Accreted Value at maturity will also bear a monetary award payable on or after maturity to the registered *or beneficial owners thereof for the benefit of students who satisfy certain eligibility criteria and are enrolled at Institutions of Higher Education (as defined herein). These Education Grant Payments are to be paid from the trust fund. See ``Higher Education Grant Program."*

Current Interest Bonds:
Aggregate Principal Amount: $38,220,000

Denominations: In denominations of $5,000 or any integral multiple thereof.

Interest Payments: Interest will be paid semiannually on July 1 and Jan. 1, commencing July 1, 1991.

Maturity: Jan. 1 in the years 1993 through 2004, inclusive.

Redemption: Subject to optional redemption prior to maturity as described herein.

Explanation: Seventy-one percent of the bonds will be structured as couponed serial bonds maturing between 2005 and 2013. These bonds will pay a fixed amount of interest twice a year. The remainder of the issue, $15.6 million, will be sold as zero coupon bonds. These "CLASS Bonds" will pay the bearer a lump sum when the securities mature or are called. In the event of a call, the value of the security is based on an accreted value schedule.

These zero coupon bonds obviously are not suitable for every investor. They are viewed as a vehicle for long-term investors who must save money to cover college tuition costs. To encourage savers, the city has set up an education grant program that provides a special bonus to students who are the beneficiary of "class" bonds.

Education Grant Amounts and Payments

Grants for the benefit of eligible students under the Education Grant Program for any current Grant Year will be in the following amounts per $5,000 Compound Accreted Value at maturity of CLASS Bonds:

Grant Amounts Per $5,000
Compound Accreted Value at Maturity

Maturity* (January 1)	Value at Maturity*	Maturity* (January 1)	Value at Maturity*
2005	$320	2010	$420
2006	$340	2011	$440
2007	$360	2012	$460
2008	$380	2013	$480
2009	$400		

The bonds will be issued pursuant to an ordinance (the "Bond Ordinance") adopted by the City Council of the City on Feb. 6, 1991, authorizing the issuance of the bonds and the levy and collection of a direct annual tax sufficient to pay the Compound Accreted Value at maturity of the CLASS Bonds and the principal of and interest on the Current Interest Bonds when due and, in connection with the bonds, authorizing certain other matters, including Education Grant Payments (as defined herein) or after maturity of the CLASS Bonds.

Explanation: Under the 1970 Illinois Constitution, the city "may exercise any power and perform any function pertaining to its government and affairs including but not limited to, the power to regulate for the protection of the public health, safety, morals and welfare; to license; to tax; and to incur debt." Unlike New York's constitution, which spells out debt limitations, Illinois does not determine the amount of bonded debt that can be incurred by home rule municipalities. The state legislature has the power to impose a limit but to date has not done so.

The issue's principal and interest payments are also secured by AMBAC insurance. The policy guarantees payment on the stated maturity dates in the case of the compounded accreted value bonds, and in the case of current interest bonds will pay interest and principal. The insurance does not cover the education grant payments. They are to be paid out of the grant program trust fund.

Economic Indicators

POPULATION STATISTICS

YEAR[1]	1979	1980	1981	1982	1983
POPULATION [2]	3,020,898	3,004,192	3,000,674	2,997,155	2,994,814
MEDIAN AGE [3]	31.2	31.1	30.4	30.7	31.0
HOUSEHOLDS[3]	1,143,700	1,138,300	1,089,300	1,102,600	1,102,400

							CHANGE
1984	**1985**	**1986**	**1987**	**1988**	**1989**	**79-89**
2,994,814	3,007,603	3,009,530	3,018,018	3,021,912	3,026,857	0.2%
31.3	31.5	31.9	32.1	32.4	32.6	4.5%
	1,122,200	1,131,200	1,135,900	1,151,500	1,153,900	0.9%

(1) Data for median age and number of households for 1990 not available as of January 31, 1991.

(2) Source: city of Chicago, Department of Planning ,estimated population. (The U.S. Census Bureau recently reported the city's 1990 population to be 2,783,726. The city's studies indicate that its population was significantly in excess of that number. The city is challenging the Census Bureau's findings, although there can be no assurance that the city will continue its challenge or that it will be successful.)

(3) Reprinted by permission of Sales & Marketing Management. Copyright August 15, 1988. "Survey of Buying Power."

Explanation: The 1990 census figures indicate Chicago's population to be about 2.9 million. Although there has been no real growth over the past 20 years, this has not affected economic growth. Unemployment continued to decline even after the October 1987 collapse of the stock market. Building permits, construction and retail sales also grew during this same period.

Retail Sales (1)

(In Millions)	*1985*	*1986*	*1987*	*1988*	*1989*
RETAIL SALES	$14,461	$14,624	$15,157	15,033	$16,076
Annual Change	1%	1%	4%	3%	6%

(1) Source: U. S. Bureau of the Census, Current Business Reports. Data for 1990 not available as of January 31, 1991.

Labor Force. Employment and Unemployment

	1985	1986	1987	1988	1989
Labor Force Participation Rate(2)	60.6%	60.6%	61.0%	60.8%	63.8%
Employment(2) (In Thousands)	1,181	1,196	1,251	1,238	1,319
Unemployment Rate (3)	9.3%	8.5%	7.7%	7.5%	7.3%

(1) Data for 1990 not available as of January 31, 1991.
(2) Source: U. S. Department of Labor, Bureau of Labor Statistics.
(3) Source: Illinois Department of Employment Security

Comparative Review of Revenues and Expenditures

Operating Funds (000)				
	1986	1987	1988	1989
Total Revenues	1,650,131	1,889,889	1,913,332	2,029,561
Total Expenditures	1,756,310	1,984,731	2,155,093	1,987,115
Fund Balances	13,434	6,119	(8,348)	42,446

Explanation: Although Chicago has experienced continuous growth in revenues, a jump in expenditures in 1987 and 1988 wiped out the fund balances. The city did react by cutting expenditures and imposing a state income tax surcharge. Revenues increased in 1989 by $40 million, which eradicated the negative fund balance and left it with a positive surplus of $12 million. By retaining the surcharge, the city expects to realize surpluses in future years.

In Chicago, taxes are not onerous, and the property tax at 10.1% of total revenues is not the predominant tax. Considering the devastating fiscal effects the 1990 recession had on most major cities, Chicago appears to be adjusting quite easily.

Debt Burden

The following table sets forth the direct and overlapping long-term debt applicable to the city as of January 31, 1991. The table does not reflect the issuance of the bonds or the refunding of the refunded bonds. Revenue bonds and notes are excluded.

Direct Debt

General Obligation Bonds (1)	$ 771,180,000
Public Building Commission Bonds (1)	22,853,600
Tender Notes (2)	550,541,000
Total Direct Debt	1,334,574,600
Less: Series 1990B and 1991B Tender Notes	438,791,000
Net Direct Long-Term Debt	905,783,600

Overlapping Debt (3)	Net Direct Debt Overlapping	Percent	Debt Applicable
Chicago Park District	$ 276,620,000	100.00%	$ 276,620,000
Chicago Board of Education	475,916,000	100.00%	475,916,000
Chicago School Finance Authority	497,005,000	100.00%	497,005,000
Community College District No. 508	264,060,000	100.00%	264,060,000
Cook County	748,80,000	43.11%	322,669,728
Cook County Forest Preserve District	7,225,000	43.11%	3,114,698
Metropolitan Water Reclamation District of Greater Chicago	$ 739,390,000	44.07%	325,849,173
Total Overlapping Debt			2,165,234,599
Total Net Direct and Overlapping Long-Term Debt			$3,071,018,19

(1) Represents the proportionate share of the principal amount of bonds issued by the Public Building Commission for projects which are secured in whole or in part by leases with the city.

(2) Tender notes issued in 1987, 1988, 1990 and January 1991, are outstanding in the amount and for the purposes shown below (table does not include Series 1991A):

Purpose	Amount	Series	Final Maturity
Equipment Purchases	$ 25,000,000	1987C	10/31/91
Equipment Purchases	36,750,000	1988C	10/31/92
Various Purposes	264,626,000	1990B	10/31/91
Equipment Purchases	30,000,000	1990C	10/31/93
Equipment Purchases	20,000,000	1990D	10/31/97
Various Purposes	174,165,000	1991B	10/31/92
TOTAL	550,541,000		

(3) Excludes outstanding GO tax anticipation notes of the city.

Explanation: Chicago operates very differently from other major cities. New York City, for example, has major departments that are part of the general fund, while Chicago has created various authorities to provide vital services. These authorities finance the services and many have their own taxing ability. Hence, to truly understand the magnitude of Chicago's debt burden, one must pay particular attention to the overlapping debt. Interesting enough, when total net direct and overlapping long-term debt is measured as a percentage of Chicago's estimated fair market property value, it is a modest 4.46%. Per capita debt is also moderate at $1,014. In contrast, New York City's 1988 per capita debt stood at $2,015 and 6.0% of property value. Also, over 60% of Chicago's debt will be paid down during the next ten years.

Chicago has maintained its A/A- rating because it appears to have a good hold on its finances during treacherous economic times. Cuts in services and the surcharge tax have resulted in surpluses, and this is certainly a superior approach to the financial gimmicks and one -shot revenue tactics employed by many other municipalities.

Determining the creditworthiness of a municipality is based on hard figures as well as a subjective analysis of the political, economic and social atmosphere of the community. Although analysts may absorb the data described in this section and come to different conclusions concerning a rating, the fundamental question they must answer is, "What is the municipality's ability to pay principal and interest on bonded debt in a timely fashion?" It should be remembered that with the exception of U.S. Government bonds, no other security in the history of finance has a greater percentage of success in being paid off in time than the general obligation bond.

Chapter 3:

Revenue Bonds: How They Work, And What to Look for Before Investing

In April 1980, *The Bond Buyer* carried an article on the "impressive rise" in the use of revenue bonds over general obligation bonds. "The traditional borrowing purposes and financing vehicles of states and localities are being supplanted by a rapid blossoming of new uses and devices that are radically altering the landscape of the municipal bond market," the article said.

The story reviewed a paper on "The Remarkable Rise of the Municipal Revenue Bond," by Ronald Forbes and Phillip Fischer of the State University of New York at Albany and John Petersen of the Government Finance Research Center. "In tracing the rapid waxing of the municipal revenue bond and the relative waning of the general obligation bond, the authors find a changing public philosophy about what activities government should finance and how they should be financed," the story noted.

The paper said, "The shared characteristic among the new issues is that while they are tax-exempt governmental obligations, they are designed to attenuate or completely sever the link between a government's ability to incur debt and its general power to levy taxes to repay such debt. In other words, the debt of the government issuer no longer is to be considered that of the taxpayer."

The paper found that what had been previously funded by the private sector through taxable borrowings was now being funded in the public sector, primarily because tax-exempt borrowing was at least 200 basis points cheaper than taxable debt. The paper gave a number of reasons for the change to revenue debt, including:

1. the expanding definition of "public purpose."

2. the unwillingness of voters to approve general obligation debt.

3. legal constraints on the use of GO debt, ranging from interest rate ceilings to tax limitations.

4. the erosion of municipal creditworthiness.

5. a desire to conduct financings in "a businesslike manner."

6. having users pay for improvements.

7. regional competition.

The change in the market specifically occurred in 1976, when for the first time the volume of revenue debt topped GO debt, $16.929 billion to $16.915 billion. In 1977, the figures changed more dramatically, to $27.17 billion revenue compared to

$17.88 billion GO; 1977 was also the first year more bonds were sold through negotiation than through the traditional process of competitive bidding, $25.03 billion to $20.02 billion. The negotiated revenue bond market has not looked back since.

Single-Family Mortgage Revenue Bonds

The general public's favorite bonded debt is undoubtedly single-family mortgage revenue bonds. The reason: The money raised by the issues has provided millions of Americans the opportunity to fulfill their dream of owning their own home. Because the bonds are self-supporting, politicians are always pleased with the programs; they can boast that they have made available low-cost mortgages without adding to the debt burden of the local governmental entity. Additional benefits provided by these programs include new jobs, growing tax bases and active real estate markets.

In 1968, Congressional legislation granted the states the power to create self-supporting authorities that could issue debt to give citizens low-interest mortgage loans. By the early 1970s, most of the states had their own agencies; in 1978, local municipalities were granted the authority to issue their own housing debt.

Any debt issued by these agencies must be self-supporting. The revenues generated from mortgage payments and reserve fund investments must be sufficient to meet all principal and interest payments.

Take a 1985 issue of the Florida Housing Finance Authority, $150 million single-family mortgage revenue bonds, Series 1. The issue bore serial coupons ranging from 5.25% in 1986 to 9.60% in 2001, and four term maturities with coupons ranging from 8.50% to 9.125%. Of this $150 million deal, $134.6 million was available to originate mortgages. The other $15.4 million was placed in a reserve fund to meet any cash-flow problems. Most issues earmark 10% to 15% for the reserve fund.

The authority's net interest cost for the borrowing was 8.83%. Eligible borrowers were charged 100 to 150 basis points above that figure; in this case, the authority had to charge borrowers 9.8% in order to have enough income to meet all principal and interest payments on the bonds. There was also a one-time charge by lending institution to the borrower of 4.5 points.

When the program commenced, the rate available to the consumer was lower than conventional mortgage rates, but that situation can easily change. General market interest rates can decline, and the mortgage rate can become unattractive. The effects of market turns will be discussed later in this section.

Other components of the single-family housing bond issue include:

• **Reserve Funds:**   Reserve money is allocated to two funds:

1) Mortgage Reserve Fund—This fund receives about 20% of available dollars and is tapped to cover loan losses.

2) Capital Reserve—It receives the remaining dollars and provides the money necessary to meet shortfalls in debt service payments.

The total reserve amounts are invested in high quality taxable securities that out-yield the interest cost of the issue.

• **Acquisition Fund:** The housing authority farms out the money to various institutions throughout its state. In the Florida case, $134.6 million was made available to local banks and savings and loans. An individual bank can purchase its allocation at an agreed-upon rate for the length of the acquisition period (and invest the money while making loans), or it can draw down portions from the authority when the loans are actually closed. The Florida deal permits the lending institution to charge 4.5% (points) as an origination fee.

The Borrower: Eligibility Rules

Banks can give loans to individuals seeking to purchase single-family houses, condominiums and duplexes. The applicant is eligible for a loan if the following federal requirements are met:

1) Residence—The applicant must sign an affidavit agreeing to occupy the residence shortly after receiving the loan; 60 days is the normal occupancy period.

2) Prior Ownership Limitation—The applicant cannot own a house nor can he have owned or had an interest in a home three years prior to the approval of a mortgage loan.

3) New Mortgage—No money from a housing issue can be used to replace an existing mortgage.

4) Purchase Price—The cost of a house may not be greater than 90% of the "average area purchase price" during the preceding twelve months. The exception is targeted areas; they can be up to 100% of the average area purchase price.

5) Mortgagor Income Limitation—Qualified applicants cannot have a family income more than 115% of the median family income of the locality or state-wide median, whichever is greater.

Mortgage Insurance

Since applicant downpayments are generally very low (5% to 10% of property value), to maintain the credibility and security of the program, issuers usually require borrowers to obtain mortgage insurance. There are basically three insurance alternatives:

1) FHA Insurance—This program is sponsored by the Department of Housing and Urban Development's Federal Housing Administration. This insurance provides the best security for mortgage principal and truly upgrades a given bond issue.

On the positive side, the insurance guarantees 100% of the unpaid principal upon foreclosure. This is paid in cash or with debentures. The payment also includes taxes and other expenses incurred by the mortgagee.

The negatives? The quality of the loans guaranteed are very low, and reimbursement on a foreclosure can take many months. When a home owner defaults, the agency can take up to a year to begin foreclosure procedures. Payment to the bank will be made only after the foreclosure is complete and the title of the property rests with HUD. If there are numerous defaults, the laborious recovery process can negatively effect the cash flow of the housing agency.

2) VA Guarantee—A veteran applying for a mortgage is eligible to receive certain guarantees from the Veterans Administration. No down payment on the house is required, and the VA will guarantee up to 60% of the mortgage. To limit exposure, the mortgage maker often insists that a private vendor or the FHA provide coverage for the part of the loan not covered by the VA.

As with FHA insurance, VA guaranteed loans are of poorer quality. Since the homeowner has no equity in the early ownership years, he has nothing to lose by walking away from his mortgage.

3) Private Mortgage Insurance (PMI)—This is a policy provided by an outside vendor and covers the piece of the mortgage loan which is in excess of 72% of the value of the house. The home owner is expected to pay the insurance premium until the loan is less than 80% of the home's value.

PMI carriers can begin foreclosure proceedings two to four months after default. When foreclosure is complete and property title is transferred to the carrier, payment of the defaulted principal balance is paid in cash.

Although private insurers react in a more timely fashion than FHA or VA, one must always be concerned with the solvency of the carrier—for, unlike the other types of insurance described, a private insurer does not have the backing of the federal government.

Additional insurance that a housing agency might require is standard homeowners insurance that covers damage from fire and special hazard insurance that covers damage from "acts of God."

Call Features of Single-Family Mortgage Bonds

One must be very careful when purchasing housing bonds, particularly older issues purchased in the secondary market. This is because it is very likely that bonds will be called for redemption prior to maturity on a regular basis; there is also the danger of large calls due to unplaced mortgage money or heavy prepayments of mortgages.

If mortgage money is not placed during the origination period (often 12 to 36 months), the remaining amount can be used to call bonds. In the case of the Florida HFA deal described earlier, the agency could have called bonds with unexpended funds at any time. That deal was dated July 6, 1985, and on July 15, 1986, $23 million in bonds were called from unexpended proceeds; another $27 million were called later in the year.

The reason for calling 30% of the issue was a dramatic drop in interest rates. The 9.8% mortgage rate offered by the agency became uncompetitive as new housing issues produced lower net interest costs.

Very few people at the beginning of 1986 anticipated a major drop in interest rates. But The Bond Buyer's 20-bond index, which stood at 8.33% on Jan. 2 , declined to 6.88% by March 13. Conventional mortgage rates fell to under 10%, and there was a great surge in mortgage refinancing and new home purchases. The mortgage rates of many housing deals sold in 1985 became suddenly unattractive, and agencies called large amounts of bonds because there was little demand for the available money.

Agencies also call bonds from cash accumulation due to early mortgage prepayments. Job transfers, death, divorce and trading up cause people to pay off their mortgages early. In the mid-1980s, prepayments were abundant because many home-owners refinanced their mortgages at substantially lower rates. Mortgage rates dropped from 16% to a low of 8.5% between 1985 and 1986.

It is fair to say that owners of housing bonds with coupons of 9.50% to 14% had their bonds called at par. The wise investor would have unloaded his bonds at a premium in anticipation of a par call.

Single Family Housing Bonds Since 1986

The concept of housing bonds is very popular; yet some members of Congress argued that the federal government was losing too much revenue as a result of this tax-exempt vehicle. There was a compromise that extended the life of single-family housing agencies but curtailed the volume of new housing issues. In 1985, new-issue volume reached a high of $37.2 billion, but by 1989 it dropped to $8.6 billion. Today, tax-exemption of housing bonds must receive Congressional approval annually.

Multifamily Mortgage Revenue Bonds

Recognizing that there was a shortage of apartments nationwide, Congress passed the landmark Housing Act of 1937. Section 11b of the act authorized the issuance of tax-exempt securities by local housing authorities and permitted federal subsidies of apartment building projects.

Over the years, many programs were implemented that failed, and numerous revisions were made to the Housing Act; nevertheless, one notion was universally accepted—federal subsidies were essential to encourage the building of projects that would benefit moderate and lower income families. In recent decades, two programs have become prominent:

1) Section 236—The government introduced this program in 1968 to subsidize developers' interest payments on new housing projects. The program failed because it merely subsidized mortgage payments but did not protect tenants during periods of rampant inflation. When the oil embargo caused home heating costs to soar, project owners were forced to pass on the increased costs, and tenants suddenly found themselves spending 40% of their incomes on rent. Many projects experienced major vacancy problems, and default became an attractive alternative because the FHA insurance guarantees made it easy for owners to just "walk away" from their properties.

In 1974, Section 236 funding was suspended and the Housing Act of 1937 was amended to permit Section 8 financing.

2) Section 8—This program provides direct rental subsidies to tenants who meet income requirements. Section 8 guarantees that a tenant will never devote more than 40% of his income to rent. Once a year, project managers are given the opportunity to prove that their building maintenance expenditures have increased. If accepted, the federal government increases tenant subsidies. This program has proven very popular, and unlike Section 236 housing projects, Section 8s have experienced very few defaults.

Although federal subsidies help tremendously in making a housing project viable, they do not remove all uncertainties. Bonds issued to build multifamily projects still contain risks that are not found in single-family issues. A multifamily housing deal is generally devoted to the building of one apartment project. Prepayment calls are highly unlikely, hence the risk of project failure looms for 30 years. Single-family mortgage bonds, on the other hand, are diversified mortgage pools that experience yearly prepayment calls and have a much shorter average life.

Additional risks holders of multifamily bonds face are:

A) Construction delays and cost overruns can doom a project.

B) Incompetent management and maintenance failure can cause tenants to vacate a building.

C) A project in a declining neighborhood can experience high vacancy levels.

Hospital Revenue Bonds

Many investors find hospital revenue bonds attractive because of their very high yields compared to other municipal bonds. But these high yields come at the price of tremendous risk. Most analysts, in fact, consider hospital credits the most difficult to follow, and the most likely to deteriorate. In 1988, for example, Standard and Poor's downgraded 12 hospitals for every one it upgraded.

Not-for-profit hospital bonds contain numerous risks because so many outside factors determine their viability. Local demographics, government policy, private insurance vendors and competition from local private hospitals all effect the finance and operations of a hospital.

Hospitals incur bonded debt to improve facilities, acquire other hospitals or refinance existing debt. They are self-supporting and must generate sufficient net revenues to meet principal and interest payments. There is no direct government bailout program, only payouts by third-party sources—federal and private insurance carriers.

Before deciding to purchase hospital bonds, the investor should review the following :

1) Five years of audited financial statements—It should be determined if there has been consistent growth in net revenues; the type of third-party reimbursements (private insurance reimbursements are more desirable than federal reimbursements); the type of accounts receivable (from individual patients or insurers).

2) Occupancy figures—A consistent increase in vacant beds may indicate a declining credit.

3) Feasibility study—Prepared by an outside consultant, the study projects the hospital's ability to meet debt service payments after a new project is completed.

4) Demographics—Declining population or a one-industry town can dramatically effect the hospital's revenue base.

5) Debt service coverage—This ratio is calculated by dividing the annual principal and interest payments into the hospital's net income, plus interest depreciation and amortization expenses. Desirable bonds should have coverage of at least two times.

Standard and Poor's describes a 1989 typical "A" rated hospital bond as follows:

Coverage of maximum annual debt service (x) 2.98
Operating income as a % of net operating revenues* 1.35
Excess income as a % of total revenues*. 3.32
Maximum debt service as a % of total revenues* 4.39
Cushion ratio (x) 4.95
Debt to plant (%) 73.61
Debt to capitalization (%) 40.24
Return on assets (%). 2.83
Cash flow (%) 17.28
Days cash on hand 99.64
Capital expense (%). 9.17

Total revenues: net operating revenues plus non-operating revenues.

It should be noted that government interference and ever-growing regulations have incredible effects on the day to day operations of a hospital. And during periods of economic retrenchment, it is likely that federal and state health subsidies will continue to decline.

College and University Revenue Bonds

To accommodate college-age baby boomers, many states created authorities that provide tax-exempt financing for public and private colleges and universities.

It is very difficult to evaluate the future of a university because to survive, it relies on the perceptions of a very small portion of the population. The university's income is derived from tuition, room and board, alumni donations, grants and endowments. The vast majority of the revenue is from tuitions; hence student enrollment and the ability to maintain sufficient student levels is the key to success.

Revenues pledged to meet principal and interest payments on bonded debt can be derived from the general obligation of the university. Since the university cannot levy taxes, this is a rather nebulous description; the ability to meet the obligation is substantially different from the traditional municipal GO. The most it can do is pledge all revenue streams to a bond issue, but there is no guarantee that this will always be sufficient. In some cases, specific revenues are dedicated to a bond project.

Income from a dormitory, plus the school's endowment revenue, for example, could be pledged to pay off the debt incurred to build that specific dormitory.

Before purchasing university bonds, past financials and the feasibility study rationalizing the proposed project should be examined. The most important factor concerning the future finances of the school is its reputation and its ability to maintain its standing as an institution of higher learning. To assess these standards, a review of the following information is essential:

1) Student- teacher ratios

2) Number of Ph.D's

3) Consistency of enrollment

4) Tuition costs compared to institutions in the area

5) Geographical diversity of the student body. A commuting college can be negatively affected by declining demographics

6) Number of research grants and the size of the research library

7) Academic quality of the students, and the dropout rate

8) Number of available programs compared to other schools in the area.

When analyzing a state controlled university, all these previously described factors must be considered, as well as the future of direct government subsidies. Recent state budget crunches have resulted in declining subsidies and increased reliance on student tuitions. This trend could be detrimental to the future of state universities because their student bodies tend to come from the ranks of lower income families. Increased tuition may prove too burdensome to these families and the number of dropouts may increase.

Student Loan Revenue Bonds

The Higher Education Act passed by Congress in 1965 contained an innovative project called the Government Insured Loan Program. To encourage lower income teens to attend college, loans could be obtained that would be 100% guaranteed by the federal government. Although there was much fanfare, the program was a disaster. Defaults were numerous, and Washington bureaucrats learned that they could not monitor the loans from the confines of the D.C. beltway.

A new system was designed in 1976 that decentralized re-sponsibilities. The new Guaranteed Student Loan Program continued to provide federal guarantees but granted the states the power to originate and monitor the loans. The states could create authorities, issue bonds, develop the collection and servicing guidelines, purchase existing loans or delegate origination powers to local banks. The federal responsibilities include:

1) Insurance guarantees—The federal government continues to guarantee loan portfolios, but to make sure that state agencies pursue recalcitrant students, it devised the following formula: On the first 5% of defaults, Washington provides 100% reimbursement; from 5% to 9% of defaults, it provides 90% reimbursement; above 9%, the government provides an 80% reimbursement. This formula reverts back to 100% each Jan. 1.

2) Federal interest subsidies—The Guaranteed Student Loan Program subsidizes interest on the loan while the student is in school and for a nine-month grace period after graduation.

3) Student Loan Marketing Association (Sallie Mae)—The government provides, for an annual fee, a vehicle that provides local agencies instant portfolio liquidity. If a cash flow short-fall develops, the local agency can sell at par to Sallie Mae the amount of loans needed to provide essential cash to meet principal and interest payments.

State agencies are self-supporting and must get their operating revenues from these sources:

1) Principal and interest payments made by   borrowers.

2) Annual federal interest subsidies.

3) Federal insurance payments on defaulted loans.

4) Cash raised by selling portfolios to Sallie Mae

5) Interest income generated from reserve fund investments.

This program has been very popular and has provided many students with the money needed to complete their university education. To be eligible, a student must be enrolled at least half time. If the undergraduate is dependent, he is eligible to receive up to $2,500 a year for four years while independent students can receive $3,000 annually. Graduate students may receive an additional $5,000 a year, but their total outstanding education loans cannot exceed $25,000.

Airport Revenue Bonds

As air travel increased in the early 1950s, the public began to demand greater access to air flight facilities. Airport authorities were created to build the appropriate fields and terminals to meet those needs. These authorities are self-supporting , and the revenue needed to meet debt service payments is generated from landing fees, which the authority charges each time a plane takes off or lands on its runways, leases signed with specific airlines for hangars and terminals, and rentals of restaurant, shop and newsstand space.

When making a decision to invest in airport revenue bonds, one must examine feasibility studies, past performance, management capabilities and local demographics. It must be determined if competitive facilities will negatively effect airport traffic. It is also desirable for the airport to have leases with several different airlines, because a strike can cripple cash flows.

Most important is the population's need for the facility. All the leases and landing fees are meaningless if there is not sufficient tourist and business traffic to encourage airline usage rates. A declining population or a one-industry community can cause airlines to abandon routes.

The Airline Deregulation Act was signed into law by President Jimmy Carter in 1978. This act produced major changes in the industry by increasing competition, opening up new routes, and closing dormant routes. It also permitted market forces to determine the cost of travel. Competitive rates encouraged the development of smaller, no-frills airlines.

Resource Recovery Revenue Bonds

Today, almost all of our municipalities are running out of space to dump garbage. Municipally owned "waste to energy," or resource recovery, plants financed with tax-exempt bonds not only alleviate the refuse problem, but create an end product—cheap energy or reusable materials.

Income needed to meet debt service payments is received from fees paid by sanitation companies to unload their trash at the resource recovery plant, proceeds from the sale of recovered products, and proceeds from the sale of energy generated by the disposal plant.

Additional revenue can be secured from "put or pay" contracts. A plant may service several municipalities, and each of these entities agrees to pay a portion of total operating and debt service payments regardless of whether or not it hauls trash to the site.

Seaport Revenue Bonds

There are over 130 seaports in the United States and most of them are run by state-created public authorities. Revenues to meet principal and interest payments are derived from leased marine terminal facilities and cargo tonnage fees. In addition, some port authorities have the backing of the local municipality's general obligation pledge.

When examining a port authority issue, it is important to know if leases have been signed for newly constructed terminals, the facility's past and projected income figures, potential labor problems, and the extent of local political interference in the day to day running of the port.

It should be noted that the activities of a port authority are not always limited to marine activities. The Port Authority of New York and New Jersey, the largest such agency in the nation, manages six marine terminals, two tunnels, two bus terminals, four bridges, four airports,and a subway system.

Toll and Gasoline Tax Revenue Bonds

Highway, bridge and tunnel construction is usually financed by tolls collected from automobile drivers who use the facility. Another way to secure revenues to meet maintenance and debt service costs is the imposition of gasoline taxes.

Before purchasing toll- and gas-tax-backed revenue bonds, the investor should determine:

1) if the issuer has the ability to raise tolls and taxes without outside political interference;

2) if there are competing toll-free roads that will attract traffic;

3) if there is a constitutional pledge by which the authority will receive the necessary portion of gasoline taxes on highway funds to meet principal and interest payments; and

4) if the authority 's debt is backed by the general obligation of the state.

Sports and Convention Center Revenue Bonds

In order to attract major league sport franchises and tourism, many communities have created sports and convention authorities that have built modern stadiums and convention facilities.

Revenues to support these projects and their bonded debt are generally derived from events held at the facilities. Additional income, if needed, is often received from the local municipalities. The Illinois Sports Facility Authority that supports the new Comiskey Park receives income from a statewide hotel tax, general fund appropriations from the city of Chicago, and an authority-levied city hotel tax. Minneapolis supports the Hubert H. Humphrey Metrodome with city liquor taxes and hotel taxes.

Sewer and Water Revenue Bonds

Sewer and water authorities provide essential services to communities throughout the nation. Usage charges levied by these authorities must generate sufficient income to meet maintenance, operational and bond principal and interest costs.

When reviewing this type of revenue bond, it should be noted if the authority is heavily dependent on federal grants, if it is in compliance with federal and state codes, if the authority can slap tax liens against those customers in arrears, and if it is mandatory for property owners to be connected to the system.

Public Power Bonds

The Public Power Act of 1930 made it possible for state and local governments to create municipal power authorities that could issue tax-exempt bonds.

During the early years of this century, public companies electrified cities because population density made it possible for them to achieve profitability rapidly. Rural America, on the other hand, was kept in the dark due to the tremendous capital needed to supply electricity to sparse populations that were stretched over thousands of miles. By the 1930s, the federal government came to believe that municipally and federally owned power could supply cheap power to these areas.

In 1933 the Congress went so far as to create the Tennessee Valley Authority. The TVA was "to improve the navigability and to provide for the flood control of the Tennessee River; to provide for reforestation and the proper use of marginal lands in the Tennessee Valley; to provide for the national defense by the creation of a corporation for the operation of Government properties at and near Muscle Shoals in the State of Alabama." The act also enumerated many specific powers, the most important one being the ability to produce, distribute and sell electric power.

Today, the TVA's electrical operations cover 91,000 square miles and supply power to municipal authorities that service over six million people in Tennessee and parts of Kentucky, Mississippi, Alabama, Georgia, North Carolina and Virginia.

Municipal power authorities are self-supporting monopolies that are confined to one state or a region within a state. There are three types of utility systems:

1) A system that creates its own electricity and maintains its own distribution center.

2) An authority that supplies power to local systems. This is often a state or regional system that encompasses numerous cities or counties.

3) A small local utility system that buys its power from a larger public or private utility.

When reviewing a public authority's financials, customer rates, future debt and building projects, the following should be considered before purchasing bonds:

1. Can the utility deliver the power needed?

2. Can the local area support the system?

3. Can rates be easily increased?

4. Are there take-or-pay contracts? Take-and-pay contracts obligate the backers to pay debt service if the plant is capable of producing any power; take-or-pay contracts require the backers to pay regardless of whether or not the plant is finished.

5. If it is a jointly owned authority, can the partners pick up the slack if one owner falters?

6. Are there fallback suppliers or systems if additional electricity is required?

Finally, there is the question of the fuel mix used to create the power. Hydroelectric power is certainly the cheapest, safest and cleanest, but many authorities are dependent on oil, gas, coal or nuclear power to create electricity.

Chapter 4:

Municipalities: What Are They? How Do They Finance Their Essential Services?

The term municipality embraces everything from a village, town, city or state to such creations as school and special districts, statutory authorities and state municipal bond banks. There are more than 83,000 of them in the U.S. according to the U.S. Census Bureau, and well over half of them have sold some sort of debt to finance everything from fire trucks to streets, bridges and highways.

Municipalities are governed by a battery of laws covering what kinds of securities they can sell, how they can sell them, for what purposes, and what kinds of securities they can invest in. During the 1980s, when Congress kept squeezing the municipal bond market by enacting more and more curbs in an effort to increase tax revenues, the ingenuity of issuers and investment bankers went into overdrive to accommodate necessary, and inevitably some abusive, municipal financings.

Before a municipal finance officer contemplates a bond issue, he puts together a capital plan. More often than not, he is faced with mounting expenses, at times declining revenues, and limited and rapidly-disappearing transfer payments from federal sources. After deciding what his particular municipality needs and what it will cost, he must decide how such necessities will be financed: whether to operate on a pay-as-you-go basis (in essence, by cash) or a pay-as-you-use basis, with bonded debt or alternative financing means. There are advantages to both approaches, but debt carries with it the promise to pay back investors, with interest. Is the municipality able and willing to pay the cost? What are the benefits to be gained by this approach, and what will be the effect on future operating budgets? And finally, what are the implications of *not* investing in the projects? There is something in the American character that still, for all its profligate ways, does not like debt. Voters in recent years have displayed less of a willingness to approve new bond issues than they had earlier.

Of course, there are ways to get around voter rejection of new bond issues. New York State, for example, found that its voters rejected bond issues for sorely-needed new prisons twice in the early 1980s. So the state, faced with a crisis in overcrowded jails, finally decided to sell revenue bonds through the Urban Development Corp. , which did not require voter approval, to build prisons.

Capital plans, then, can range from whether or not to build a new prison or a wing to a school, to figuring out how much it will cost for new subway cars and how to pay for them, to figuring out what pieces of an entire state's infrastructure need to be repaired, and how to pay for them.

The Checklist: Bringing an Issue to Market

Once he has decided to sell debt, the finance officer faces a checklist of things to do. He must decide whether or not to hire a financial adviser, when to schedule a bond issue for sale, how to structure it, and whether to sell bonds through competition or negotiation. He also picks a bond counsel and a fiscal agent. If he decides on the negotiated route, he also chooses an underwriter.

The finance officer also has to worry about the issuer's place in the market and how its credit is perceived by investors and by rating agencies, and about disclosing details of the issuer's financial condition. These are on top of his concerns about taxes and revenues, investment income and, of course, his own livelihood, if he is an elected official.

About 10 years ago, few issuers used financial advisers; now, in mute testimony to how complicated life has become for all but the most sophisticated issuers, about 80% do.

There has been some question in recent years whether municipalities should hire independent financial advisers or those who also buy and sell bonds as a dealer.

J. Chester Johnson, president of his own financial advisory firm and founder of the National Association of Independent Financial Advisors in 1989, said on the organization's founding that he thought independent advisers could better provide service to the issuer without the conflict of interest inherent in having an adviser also trade and sell bonds and who might, after acting as financial adviser on an issue, bid on the issuer's bonds and underwrite them.

Representatives of financial advisers who work for dealers, on the other hand, counter that maintaining trading and un-derwriting departments means that they are on top of market conditions and thus can best advise municipalities on when and how to issue their bonds. The biggest financial advisers in the field, not surprisingly, belong to dealers, who have the most money to commit to their various activities.

Either way, unless the municipality comes to market more than four or five times a year and its own finance director is extremely sophisticated —such as, for example, New York's Metropolitan Transportation Authority—the first step should be to hire a financial adviser. According to the late Lennox Moak's invaluable *Municipal Bonds: Planning, Sale, and Administration* (1982), the financial adviser helps the issuer in at least 11 ways:

1. Making a presentation to rating agencies.

2. Helping to calculate the timing of a bond sale.

3. Determining the range of interest costs for different alternative potential means of financing.

4. Determining the reasonableness of fees for other specialized services.

5. Providing an idea of what underwriters' fees should be.

6. Deciding upon call provisions suitable for the bond issue.

7. Structuring the bond issue.

8. Setting bidding requirements and other terms of public sale or

9. Helping to conduct a negotiated sale.

10. Evaluating the sale when it is finished.

11. Evaluating the performance of each of the members of the syndicate in a negotiated financing.

Coming to Market: Negotiated or Competitive?

A municipality sells debt either through negotiation, in which case it deals with a sole underwriter or underwriting syndicate to set the interest rates and terms of the deal, including maturity structure; or through competition, when the municipality takes bids at auction for its securities.

The Government Finance Officers Association believes it is in the best interests of the issuer to go the competitive route most of the time. In its 49-page handbook, *An Elected Official's Guide to Government Finance*, which has gone through six printings since its publication in 1984, the association urges, "Competitive sales should be used to market debt whenever feasible."

The GFOA further notes, "For certain large, irregular and difficult-to-place issues, negotiated underwriting may be necessary. If negotiation is used, special care must be taken to ensure that underwriter profits reflect genuine risks." Finally, with somewhat adversarial overtones, the association says, "Competitive underwriter selection is recommended, and independent financial advisers may be necessary to monitor the underwriter. *Negotiated underwritings can be extremely profitable for securities dealers; governments should seek to ensure that such profits are reasonable"*(italics ours).

Yet for all of this, negotiated financings have proven more popular over the past decade, and there is no reason to think they will become otherwise. During the past 10 years, the sector of the market sold through competition, most often general obligation bonds, was remarkably stable, running anywhere from 20% to 35% of the market. The sector of the market that really exploded throughout the period was the negotiated revenue bond market—generally larger, more complicated project financings that in general did not have to be approved by voters.

In 1979, $42.21 billion in bonds were sold, comprising $23.57 billion in negotiated sales and $18.64 billion competitive. Revenue bonds accounted for nearly $30 billion of the total. In 1982, total volume rose to $77.17 billion, with $51.61 billion of that negotiated; $53.90 billion of all bonds sold were revenue bonds. By 1984, because of the threat of tax reform, volume increased to $101.88 billion, with nearly $75 billion of that revenue debt, and $75 billion negotiated.

The year 1985, the record year for the market, is generally regarded by market participants as an aberration, fueled by wild speculation, much of it correct, about the effects of the Tax Reform Act of 1986. Long-term volume hit $204.28 billion, $148.99 billion of that revenue bonds, $162.79 billion negotiated. The negotiated-revenue composition of municipal bond volume continues to range around 20% of the total volume figure.

Critics of negotiated financing may be alarmed, but banker Mark Ferber of Lazard Freres & Co., one of the nation's top financial advisers, explains how issuers benefit from negotiated sales.

"The most important reason for an issuer to go negotiated is that a negotiated sale can respond to nuances in the marketplace, and in marketing," he said. "With a competitive sale, which relies on a predetermined structure, you cannot. If the market moves, so that the calendar is crowded and you have a significant number of zero-coupon bonds on the calendar, for example, you may want to restructure your transaction.

"With a negotiated sale, you assist the issuer. In the case of a refunding, you maximize savings to the issuer. In the case of a new-money sale, with tax-exempt and taxable portions, you maximize the tax-exempt portion. Many transactions simply cannot be structured in advance.

"Finally, in a negotiated sale, two fundamental services can be performed for the issuer: marketing and sale of the bonds; and preparation for the marketing and sale of the bonds, such as documentation and presentation to the rating agencies, and providing critical responses to buyer's questions."

Ferber said he thought that, in the 1990s, with more complicated structures and more difficult markets, "it is incorrect to presume that a competitive deal will provide the best rate for the issuer."

Ferber summed up the argument for negotiation in a chapter written for the GFOA's own manual, *The Price of Advice* (1986). If its bond issue was large and required aggressive retail marketing, if it was concerned about timing or the structure or the complexity of the deal, or even if the financing was being done by a new issuer or new administration, then the issuer might consider negotiation.

But as California showed in 1991, size need not be a consideration. The state came to market in February with a $1.3 billion general obligation bond issue, the largest competitive deal ever, and received the lowest true interest cost on a California GO in 10 years.

Default and Disclosure

Short of a natural disaster, the worst thing that can happen to a municipal issuer is that it defaults, or fails to make principal and interest payments on its debt.

Fortunately for investors and issuers, default is a rare event. It has been estimated that less than one-half of 1% of all municipal issues default, and that the odds of default are about four in 10,000. The most likely issues to default, experience has shown, are small health care issues, industrial development bonds, and tax increment bonds issued by special districts dependent upon development to pay back debt.

While it is true that most defaults are small, and often quickly remedied, two notable ones demonstrate the need for buyers to research any issue in which they are considering investing, and for issuers to adequately disclose their finances. The collapse of New York City in the 1970s led to the rise of municipal bond analysis as a profession and to the improvement of the official statement, the offering prospectus for an issuer's securities. Official statements have grown larger and larger and now include not only such details as a description of the securities to be offered in regard to maturities and interest rate structures, but also budgetary information, financial projections, engineers' reports (in the case of specific projects), and descriptions of legal matters.

Even with this added information, however, investors were stung by the WPPSS default. Subsequently, the SEC, under pressure from Congress and others to punish all those connected with the WPPSS projects 4 and 5 bond issues, in 1988 created a new rule designed to ensure that investors would receive timely information on an issuer's financial situation.

The SEC's new rule in essence states that municipalities selling issues of $1 million or more are required, with certain exemptions, to provide underwriters with nearly complete official statements before they issue bonds. Whether this rule would have affected the outcome of the WPPSS situation is a matter for debate — a WPPSS executive once noted, before the agency began a refinancing of $2 billion of high-coupon debt sold for projects 1 and 3, "We feel there's nothing in there that we haven't already been doing."

It seems likely that increased disclosure will be a fact of life for thousands of issuers who have never given a thought to such matters, except when they have come to market to sell bonds.

The SEC noted in a lengthy discussion of its rule in 1990 that "among frequent issuers, the quality of disclosure was reported to be quite good." It added: "The Public Securities Association noted, for example, that most of those responding to its survey of current disclosure practices in the municipal markets had rated disclosure practices in new issues as 'satisfactory' and 'very good.' It pointed out that 94% of those responding to the survey rated 'content and completeness' of disclosure documents in new issues as 'satisfactory' to 'excellent.' Nevertheless, the PSA reported that this very positive assessment of disclosure practices dropped sharply when the availability of disclosure was considered." The PSA said that 45% of those responding to its survey rated availability of documents in a timely fashion as less than satisfactory.

"The views of the PSA generally correspond to the comments received from issuers, underwriters and investors," the SEC continued. "While most issuers are conscientious about providing adequate quantities of official statements in a timely fashion, commentators indicated that there was a range of practices. Investors, in particular, have complained about the ability to obtain disclosure documents prepared by issuers at a time that would permit review prior to making an investment decision."

In addition, the SEC said, underwriters who did not want to run afoul of antifraud provisions in federal securities laws said they wanted to review disclosure of infrequent issuers before recommending their bonds for investment.

The SEC summed up its comments: "The Commission believes that Rule 15c2-12 will promote industry professionalism and confidence in the integrity of the municipal markets without burdening issuers." *(For further information on the push for more disclosure, see Chapter IX, "The Regulators.")*

The sticking point, according to market observers, is that disclosure requirements are hardly new. The Government Finance Officers Association promulgated such rules in 1975; the National Federation of Municipal Analysts spelled out what it wanted in the way of disclosure in 1988. As one financial analyst put it, "Infrequent issuers who come to market every five years will still balk at providing regular information. It's the issuer's document, all right, but the underwriters, subject to disciplinary action by the SEC, will be the impetus for action on disclosure. There is no *rule* for the issuers to provide anything, and no punishment if they don't."

A recent case in point should suffice. In May 1988, Moody's Investors Service pulled its ratings on 447 issuers, saying the municipalities were uncooperative in providing the rating agency with financial information. Officials of the municipalities in question said that since they sold bonds so infrequently, there was no need for them to submit financial information to the rating agency, and what's more, that Moody's should have tried to get the information on its own.

Chapter 5:

Municipal Bond Underwriting: Competitive Sale

The previous chapter examined how a municipality makes the decision to issue bonds: a local ruling body perceives a need to incur bonded debt, it receives voter approval, it complies with state constitutional and finance law, and it hires a financial adviser who prepares an official statement and sends out the official notice of sale to prospective buyers of the issue.

This section will describe how a bond is sold through competitive bidding and the events that transpire between the time the sale notification is put in the mail and the awarding of the bonds to the winning underwriting syndicate. To add life to these events, an actual deal, by New York's Suffolk County, located in eastern Long Island, will be reviewed step by step.

Notice of Sale

In New York State the vast majority of local general obligation bond deals come to market via the competitive route because the local finance laws insist upon it. There are certain exceptions, like New York City and Buffalo, which because of their fiscal woes during the 1970s could not easily sell bonds through competitive bidding, but most bonds come to market this way.

A mailing is prepared by the municipality's chief financial officer or financial adviser and sent to prospective bidders and to *The Bond Buyer,* which lists it in its new bond offerings section. The package contains the notice of sale, the preliminary official statement and the bid form. Bidders for small offerings — those under $30 million — are usually regional broker-dealers and dealer banks. In New York State, Roosevelt & Cross and Chemical Bank head up the bulk of successful underwriting syndicates.

What follows is a review and explanation of the information provided in Suffolk County's notification package:

Issuer : County of Suffolk, New York
Sale Date: 5/22/90
Time: 11:30 a.m. (EDST)
Purpose: Public Improvement Serial Bonds
1990 Series A : Unlimited Tax
Serials : 1991 to 2015
Amount:— $21,280,000

Denomination: $5,000
Registration: Book Entry
Good Faith Deposit: $425,600

Explanation: Suffolk County announces on May 10, 1990, that it will entertain bids to raise $21.2 million on Tuesday, May 22, at 11:30 a.m. The money will be used to provide various capital improvements throughout the county. Payment is guaranteed by the unlimited taxing authority of the municipality — in other words, it can raise property taxes as high as it must in order to pay principal and interest on the borrowed debt.

The deal will be structured with serial bonds that will mature yearly from 1991 to 2015. Serial bonds permit the borrower to amortize its debt over a number of years. Issues structured with a term bond, on the other hand, have the bulk of the loan come due in one year. The Suffolk bonds will be in denominations of $5,000.

In the past, when bearer bonds were issued, an investor purchasing $100,000 par amount of bonds would physically receive 20 $5,000 bonds with attached coupons. To collect the interest, the holder would clip the coupons from each bond on the appropriate payment date and then cash them at a branch of the paying agent. Since 1983, bond issues are registered "book entry," meaning that an appointed depository holds the securities on behalf of the owner. The owner instead receives a certificate with his name registered on it. Instead of coupons, the owner automatically receives an interest check twice a year from the paying agent.

To ensure that a bidder is serious, a good faith check of $425,600 (2% of the face amount is normal) must accompany the underwriter's bid .

Dated: 5/1/90
Due: 4/1/91 to 2015
First Interest: 4/1/91

Explanation: The bond's issue date, or "dated date," is the day from which the owner starts accruing interest. In the Suffolk County issue, interest begins accruing on May 1, 1990, even though the deal does not actually settle until May 30.

The due date is the day on which the serial bonds begin to mature. On April 1, 1991, the first of the serial bonds will come due, and every April 1 thereafter until 2015 a portion of the bonds will be retired. In 1991, $685,000 Suffolk County bonds will mature, and the amount will go up slightly every year, with $1,015,000 maturing in the year 2015.

The first interest payment on the Suffolk issue is unusually long, eleven months after the dated date. In most issues, the first interest payment is five or six months after the issue date. Investors who buy this bond must be cognizant of the long payment date, particularly if they are dependent on the income.

Bid Specifications

All or None — Yes
Number of Rates — 25
Coupon Cannot Exceed (N.X.) — 8.75%
Multiples — 1/8 or 1/20 of 1%
Par — Not less than par
Other Limits — Rates for Bonds due 2001-2015 must be in nondescending order; rate differential, 2%; one rate per maturity.

Explanation: For the layman, this is where it gets complicated. A seasoned underwriter, however, can easily cut through this jargon when formulating a bidding strategy.

In the Suffolk County deal, the successful bidder must buy the entire deal — "all or none" — and be willing to take on the entire $21,280,000 loan. It cannot bid for a portion of the issue, as can be done with short-term note deals.

There will be 25 maturities; if it makes sense mathematically, there could be 25 different coupons. The financial adviser or the county comptroller has determined that it does not want a coupon higher than 8.75%. Coupons can be in multiples of 1/8 (.125 basis points) or 1/20 (.05 basis points) of 1%. These multiples can vary, but in this case the underwriter is given the most latitude in selecting coupons.

Coupons for bonds maturing between 2001 and 2015 can only increase; they cannot decrease. For example, bonds maturing in 2001 would have a 6.10% coupon, bonds due the following year would have a 6.20% coupon, and so on. If a prospective underwriter bid the 2001 bonds with a 6.20% coupon and the

2002 bonds with a 6.10% coupon, that would defy the bid instructions and this bid would be thrown out by the municipality.

Also, the issuer will not accept a discount bid; it wants to receive from the buyer of the bonds the entire $21.28 million.

Finally, the difference in the coupon structuring can be no more than 2%. This means that if the lowest coupon is 6%, the highest coupon cannot exceed 8%. This limitation often appears because the issuer wants to avoid a large discount coupon at the end of the deal.

Call Features

Bonds due 2001-2015 are callable as a whole or in part in inverse order of maturity or in equal proportionate amounts on any interest payment date on and after 4/1/00, at the following prices plus accrued interest: 102% if called 4/1/00 and 10/1/00; 101% if called 4/1/01 and 10/01/01; 100% if called 4/1/02 and thereafter.

Explanation: In this loan, the bonds due 1991 through 2000 are noncallable. Holders of these bonds are protected because the issuer cannot call the bonds prior to maturity under any circumstances.

There is no protection, however, from 2001 on out. If interest rates are lower in any of those years than that which Suffolk County is paying out, the county may be tempted to call all outstanding bonds and refinance at lower prevailing rates. Those investors who purchase bonds in the callable range do receive a slight premium if their securities are called in 2000 (102% of par value) or 2001 (101% of par value); but starting in 2002, all bonds are callable at par. If there is a call, the longest bonds must be called first, or there must be equal amounts called in each maturity.

Basis of Award: True Interest Cost

Explanation: The TIC method (also known as Canadian Interest Cost) includes the total dollar amount of interest payments and the timing of principal and interest payments. The TIC takes into consideration the time value of money, hence the figure is slightly higher than the other widely used method of calculating interest cost, known as Net Interest Cost. The NIC is the total amount of interest payments made during the life of the loan.

Paying Agent: The Depository Trust Company of New York (DTC)
Legal Opinion: Willkie Farr and Gallagher
Delivery: On or about 5/30/90 at the office of bond counsel.

Explanation: The securities issued by Suffolk County will be deposited with the Depository Trust Co. The owners of the bonds will be listed by book entry at DTC and will receive interest checks on April 1 and October 1 each year.

The legal opinion stating that the issue complies with existing statues and, most importantly, that interest is exempt from federal taxation, will be issued by the distinguished municipal bond counsel firm of Willkie Farr and Gallagher.

The entire bond deal is slated to settle on or about May 30, 1990, at the offices of the bond counsel. At that meeting, Suffolk County receives its $21.280 million and the purchaser, the underwriter with the winning bid, receives the bond certificates.

The Underwriting Syndicate

Prospective underwriters receive the notification of sale from Suffolk County or read the sale announcement in *The Bond Buyer.* Throughout Wall Street, underwriters at various firms start files on the deal and distribute this information to their trading desks and sales forces, and direct their research departments to check on the creditworthiness of the issuer. Sales managers bring the deal to the attention of institutional and retail salesmen — Suffolk County bonds are generally purchased by individual investors. The salesmen report back on the interest they are seeing among customers and the interest rates at which they think they can sell bonds. Firms also call each other to discuss banding together in a syndicate to bid on the deal, rather than bid on the issue by themselves.

At Chemical Bank the book running manager of what will be the successful syndicate, Lou Sprauer, manager of the underwriting department, directs an assistant underwriter to mark the sale date on the firm's calendar and looks through the bank's file on Suffolk County for historical information on past county bond sales, such as interest rates on previous deals and which firms have underwritten these issues.

The Lead Underwriter

The lead underwriter manages the books and takes care of all the paper work and regulatory reporting for the syndicate. This underwriter may have headed the same group for past bond issues by the municipality or it may have rotated the managing spot with another firm.

The syndicate contract is sent out to all members of the group. It lists managers, joint managers, major and minor members, their potential liabilities, and the time and place of the syndicate meetings. On occasion, a new dealer may ask to join a syndicate. The manager may independently make the decision to admit the new member or, if it is politically sensitive, consult with the other major members of the group.

In addition, a member in the lower tier may ask to be moved up permanently to a higher bracket — which, if granted, obligates him to take on greater liability with the hopes of getting a bigger portion of syndicate profits. When making a decision, managers examine members' past account per-formance to determine whether a promotion will add any strength to the group.

Other information included in the syndicate letter:
1) The rules setting the offering terms
2) Liabilities and expenses of members
3) Rights and powers of the syndicate manager
4) The duration of the account
5) The priority of orders received by the syndicate.

The type of account is also spelled out in the contract. There are two types:
1) Eastern Contract: This is the most popular type of syndicate account and it is universal in the eastern part of the U.S. In this account, a participant's liability is undivided. Even though a member may take down and sell bonds greater in number than its participation, it still has a proportional li-ability for the number of unsold bonds left in the account.

For example, an underwriter has a 10% participation in a $1 million deal, but sells $200,000 of bonds, or twice its participation. If the remaining $800,000 in the syndicate goes unsold, the underwriter is still obligated to take down 10% of that, or another $80,000 of bonds. If the remainder of the deal goes unsold and the syndicate is forced to take a loss, the underwriter must pay up his proportionate share. If the loss is $50,000, the underwriter must come up with 10% of that loss, or $5,000. On the other hand, if this underwriter sells no bonds and the account makes money, he is still entitled to 10% of the profits.

2) Western Contract: In this type of account, the liability is divided. If a member participates in 10% of the deal, and sells 10%, then it has no other liability. If the member has sold only 5% and the deal loses money, it will have to come up with only 5% of the loss. Also, if the deal breaks up, the member is handed his proportion of the remaining bonds. This account procedure is rare and surfaces occasionally in the central states.

In the group headed by Chemical Bank, there are 26 members, of which 13 are joint managers. The Suffolk deal actually consists of two parts totalling $77.7 million; the managers thus each take on $6 million in liability. There are also two associated members (these are often smaller bidding groups that merge with a larger syndicate) that have $6 million participations. Finally, the 13 second tier underwriters are each assigned $1 million in liabilities.

If all the members stay in the underwriting, the syndicate participation will be "over-underwritten" by $25.3 million. The proportional liability share could decrease if there are no dropouts from the group.

Designing the Winning Bid

The underwriters' objective is to put together a maturity scale and coupons that are within the issuer's bid limitations and yet result in the lowest true interest cost to the issuer, while leaving themselves room to make a profit.

The various syndicates hold preliminary pricing meetings late in the afternoon on the day before the sale. In a major deal with many syndicate members, there is a formal meeting at the office of the book-running manager; for smaller underwritings, the manager keeps in touch with the other members by telephone. This meeting gives the manager the opportunity to feel out the other members concerning their market views, overall buying interest, and to sketch a scale of maturities and coupons. The indications procured give the manager the raw materials essential to begin work on syndicate mathematics.

The final meeting commences about one hour before the bids are due. At Chemical Bank, Sprauer, the underwriting manager, enters a small auditorium, calls the meeting to order and reads out a maturity scale, coupons and orders from investors he has in hand based on those numbers. The other underwriters digest his proposal.

A poll is taken and members of Chemical's syndicate give their views and pre-sale orders from their customers. Representatives from the various underwriting firms then flock to the telephones to give their trading desks the proposed scale and to find out if there are any additional orders from customers. Based on the feedback, the syndicate manager may adjust the scale to make the other members more comfortable with the deal or to shore up a fence-sitting buyer. At this time, the spread, or the amount of profit for which the syndicate will work, is determined.

A final roll call is then taken and each member must decide if he wants to commit his firm's capital to the underwriting. If it is a hot deal (if there are pre-sale orders for most of the bonds) then the decision is easy, since it looks like a money-maker for the firm. When the underwriter hears his firm's name called out, he gives one of four replies:

1) "O.K." — This means he's in the deal, and if a number of underwriters drop out of the syndicate, he is willing to take on his proportional share of additional liability, regardless of the amount.

2) "O.K. up to an 'X' amount" — The underwriter agrees to stay in but wants to limit his potential increase in liability. For instance, if the member is in for $1 million in a $10 million deal, he may tell the manager, "O.K. up to $2 million." This means he is willing to help the syndicate to buy the bonds by doubling his share of the liability, if necessary.

3) "O.K., no more" — The member will participate in the deal but refuses to take on any additional liability.

4) "Sorry, No" — This is the most difficult response; it means the member is dropping out of the account and is absolved of any liability. When the words "Sorry, No" are heard, the person

saying them is usually staring down at the floor — it is the ultimate humiliation for an underwriter.

Why does an underwriter drop out of a syndicate? The underwriter may not like the market; he may perceive that the deal is going to be a dog and doesn't want to take a loss; his boss may have told him to drop from the account. Remember, in a competitive deal, the winning account immediately owns the bonds and is subject to market risks. If he buys the bonds from the issuer but then can't sell them to his customers, he's stuck with them and may even have to sell them at below cost to get rid of them. An underwriter may sense some pending doom and may not want to be part of a deal that might be "under water" (selling at a loss) before he gets back to his office.

Sometimes an underwriter, as a result of syndicate politics, may not be able to afford the luxury of dropping out. A firm may have been recently moved up from a minor bracket to a major bracket — meaning it now can demand more bonds in the syndicates it enters — and feels it can't drop out because it will look ungrateful or unworthy of the new role. Or a major may be a rotating manager and must constantly show his support for the group.

In the Chemical Bank group bidding on the Suffolk County issue, all the original majors stayed in the deal, four new majors joined the account, and one member moved up to a joint manager.

The Bids Are Opened

At precisely 11:30, the comptroller or financial adviser opens the bid envelopes and determines who has bid the lowest true interest cost. If the comptroller is happy with the winning TIC, he will award the deal; if not — say all of the bids are too high — he has the option to reject all bids. Generally, a few minutes before the deal goes off, the competing underwriting groups compare notes and are able to figure out which of them has won before the award is official.

A bidding group could be late in delivering its bid and as such is disqualified; it has happened in deals big and small. In this event, the cover bid, or second-best bid, is awarded the deal. But it occasionally happens that a late bid is also the lowest. In this case, there is total chaos as salesmen scramble to the telephones to inform prospective buyers.

Sometimes, when there is a wide cover between the late bid and the runner-up, the issuer will exercise its right to reject all bids and reschedule the deal. Taking this route presents the issuer with additional costs and risks. The municipality must send out new sales notices, which costs money, but more important is the potential market risk. During the period between the two bids, the market could go against the issuer and it could wind up paying a higher interest cost than that of the original cover bid.

Underwriters can also make mistakes on their bid forms, such as, for example putting 1% where they meant to put 7%. Issuers normally reject obvious clerical errors like this, but legally they could hold the underwriters to honor their bid. Underwriters, however, have the option in a situation like this to walk away from the deal, thus forfeiting their good faith check.

In the Suffolk deal, the winning underwriters' strategy was to place the maximum coupon, 8.75%, up front (1991 to 1998). This produced premium bonds which contained potential profit for the syndicate. The profit here is the difference between par (100) and the premium dollar paid. The remainder of the bonds (1999 through 2015) are priced at par or a slight discount and contribute nothing to the syndicate's total spread.

In this underwriting, Suffolk County received the par amount , or $21,280,000. The gross production (which includes premiums) was $21,718,725.75. The spread was $436,240.

The spread (the amount of money that remains with the syndicate) contains four elements:

1) Expenses — the cost incurred by the syndicate manager for ordinary expenses.

2) Management Fee — the amount that goes to the manager for running the entire deal.

3) Takedown — this consists of the "concession" and the "additional takedown." It is the total takedown that goes to a member for taking ownership of the bonds of a given maturity.

In the Suffolk deal, the 1991 bonds had a total takedown of $12.50 per bond ($7.50 concession plus $5.00 additional takedown). On 100 bonds , or $100,000, then, the takedown is $1,250.

4) Remainder — Money left in the account will be distributed proportionately (based on liability) to the members of the syndicate. This assumes that the bonds in the syndicate are

actually sold at a profit and that money still remains in the account.

The Suffolk County account led by Chemical Bank worked for $20.50 per $1,000 bond. The average takedown was $10.585 leaving $9.91 per bond. This remainder is used for expenses (about $1.00 per bond) and profit distributions among the participating firms.

The Order Period

After the deal is awarded, the successful group usually has about an hour to take orders from its customers. During this time, the members work the deal and solicit orders for the remaining bonds.

To avoid fist fights and worse when it comes to bond allocations among the underwriters, the Municipal Securities Rulemaking Board has established priority guidelines that obligate each of the underwriters to disclose the nature of their sales .

After the allocation of bonds, based on member orders, an account will often still have unsold bonds. The managing underwriter advertises them in the *Blue List* and hopes that dealers throughout the country are hungry for the bonds. If an account member wants bonds, it gets them at the total takedown; if a non-member purchases bonds, it gets them at the concession. This scenario can, however, change: If the market deteriorates, the account may unload the bonds at the takedown to any buyer. Also, to clean out an account, the underwriter might entertain "down" bids, or a price below the break even cost. If this comes to pass, the manager might poll the majors to make sure he has support for his intended action.

Once the account is closed and all the bonds are sold, the remaining chores are administrative. The Suffolk deal settled on May 30, 1990. On that day the county received its money, the members received their bonds and in turn delivered them to the buyers. The managing underwriter completes the paper work in accordance with MSRB rules, determines the remaining profit in the account, and cuts checks for each underwriter based on its proportionate share. If the account lost money, the members send a check covering their proportional share of that loss to the manager.

The Secondary Market

When underwriters close their books on deals, the life of the bonds goes on in the secondary market. The players who oversee this aspect of the municipal industry are an extraordinary collection of eccentrics called bond traders, professionals who buy and sell blocks of bonds for their firm's sales force.

A typical trader's day works in the following fashion, whether he works in the general market or specializes in notes, GO bonds, revenue bonds, sinking fund issues, "special situations," retail or institutional business.

The trader arrives at his desk around 7:00 or 7:30 a.m. and scans the daily newspapers, including *The Bond Buyer,* then studies the *Blue List,* once serendipitously referred to as a "bond novel." The *Blue List,* formally called the *Blue List of Current Municipal Bond Offerings,* so-called because of the pale blue paper it is printed on, lists bonds and notes being offered by dealers, and includes their par value, issuer, maturity date, coupon and price or yield, as well as who is offering them. By studying the *Blue List,* one can determine where supply is in the market.

The trader then turns his attention to his various screens, including Bloomberg, Telerate, the Dow Wire and the Munifacts newswire, which also includes long lists of offerings like the *Blue List.*

Four things will inform the rest of the trader's day. He will speak with his salesmen, finding out where demand is in the market at that moment; work the telephones, discussing the market with other traders; watch the various financial indicators that are released by government departments and try to divine what they mean for his market; and watch for other news that might affect the market, including the introduction of new tax legislation, ratings downgrades, Federal Reserve Board activity in the government bond market, and the like.

What the authors of a chapter in the *Municipal Bond Handbook,*Daniel Delahanty and Alan Goldstein, then of Bear, Stearns & Co., wrote in 1983 still rings true today: "The trader must constantly try to generate activity. His function is basically to buy and sell securities and turn over his position as quickly as possible. No trader should ever take a long-term view about a bond. He has to be able to appreciate only a certain moment in time and utilize it to its fullest."

Chapter 6:

Municipal Bond Underwriting: Negotiated Sale

During the past 15 years, the municipal market has undergone a sea change. Before, the market consisted mostly of general obligation bonds sold through competitive bidding. Now, the predominant means of raising money for tax-exempt projects is revenue bonds sold to underwriters through negotiation. In 1976, for the first time, negotiated deals were responsible for about 60% of the par value of bonds issued; in 1989, more than 75% of the money raised was through negotiation.

The mechanics for a negotiated sale are quite simple: A municipality hires an underwriter to structure a deal and to price it to sell. Issuance expenses are typically greater for a negotiated deal than a competitive sale because the underwriter in a negotiated offering charges a management fee for its services. The underwriter may spend hundreds of hours structuring the deal and marketing it to investors in order to get the best price for the issuer.

A history of average gross underwriting spreads can be seen in the attached table.

Why municipalities might be willing to pay for this service was discussed in Chapter 4, "The Municipality." As the GFOA put forth in its 1984 *An Elected Official's Guide to Government Finance,* negotiated financings should be used only for "large, irregular and difficult-to-place issues."

Bankers are sharply divided over the question of which method, competitive or negotiated, is best. Some say negotiation encourages the greedy to get greedier. As one banker put it: "In the final analysis, with competitive bids, you save the taxpayer money. But the only way the dealer really makes money is through negotiation."

A proponent of the competitive process notes, "We know what happens when the Pentagon doesn't take bids: you wind up with $94 hammers," while other bankers note that competitive underwriting saves money in the short term. But others testify that the shrewd price structuring and timing inherent in negotiated deals makes for bigger savings in the long run.

Girard Miller, now a vice president of government markets at Fidelity Investments, a top buyer of municipal bonds and author of the GFOA booklet, said he still believes what he wrote in 1984. "Nothing has changed," he said. "There's still the potential for political abuse with negotiation. Competitive sales on plain vanilla deals are still the preferable way to go. On negotiated issues, you have to worry about the back-slapping and arm-twisting that brought the deal in the door."

Suffice it to say, then, that in today's market, many dealers are not anxious to commit their capital to a huge competitive deals and consequently urge their clients to go the negotiated route. With narrow profit spreads, a sudden market turn can cost a major underwriter a year's bonus if it is caught with a large inventory of competitive deals that will not move.

Negotiated offerings differ from competitive deals in that the transfer of bond ownership does not take place until the deal is completely sold. If a negotiated deal is hot or oversubscribed — orders being greater than the size of the deal — it can be repriced upward — that is, with lower interest rates — to save the issuer money. If the deal is slow, the scale can be changed to provide higher yields until there is enough interest to sell out the entire issue.

When the issue is sold, the underwriter presents the pricing to the municipality, which then "awards" the deal. The underwriter then allocates the bonds to the various members of the syndicate based on earlier orders. Since the underwriter doesn't automatically own the bonds, as it does in a competitive deal, the market has time to digest the underwriting.

Because this form of finance is lucrative to investment banking firms, public finance departments throughout the dealer community actively and aggressively seek top underwriting management positions. Theoretically, a municipality invites various investment banking firms to submit proposals for an upcoming financing. Those with the best ideas and lowest fees are named as members of an underwriting group. There are senior managers and lower tiers of underwriters, and last of all, a selling group, comprising dealers who receive securities, less the selling concession, from the syndicate managers.

Politics and Money

When new administrations take office in a municipality, they usually choose new underwriting syndicates for their bonds. Criteria for the selection include the dealers' amount of capital, their ability to sell bonds, whether they sell primarily

Gross Spreads: 1982-91

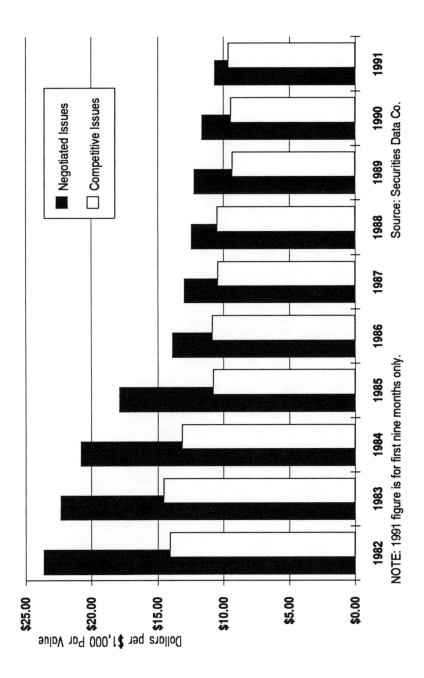

Negotiated Issues

Competitive Issues

Dollars per $1,000 Par Value

$25.00
$20.00
$15.00
$10.00
$5.00
$0.00

1982 1983 1984 1985 1986 1987 1988 1989 1990 1991

NOTE: 1991 figure is for first nine months only.

Source: Securities Data Co.

to institutional or retail clients, and their reputation and fiscal probity. For example, during the 1980s, E.F. Hutton & Co. lost a lot of underwriting business after it admitted guilt in a check-kiting scheme. This eventually led to its demise. Similarly, municipalities refused to do business with Drexel Burnham Lambert when it pleaded guilty to malfeasance in its junk bond deals.

Then there are the unspoken things that go into underwriter selection: politics and money.

Those firms who get deals are frequently those with "political acumen," as one banker characterized it. "The competitive advantage," he said, "is politics." Jesse Unruh, late treasurer of California, summed up the situation when he said, "Money is the mother's milk of politics."

Politics can range from requiring the presence on an underwriting team of minority- or women-owned investment banking or bond counsel firms to doing business with friends' or relatives' firms.

Money is self-explanatory — municipal bond business, in many instances, goes to the firms that give the most in campaign contributions to winning candidates. One New York banker noted, "It's gotten to the point where senior people are coughing up $15,000 and more and spending half their time at fund-raisers" as part of the price of doing business and winning good spots on underwriting syndicates.

Firms can easily circumvent legal limits on campaign contributions by having their employees give as individuals. They either do so voluntarily, or because they are advised to do so by their employers. In some cases, firms deduct a certain amount from their employees' paychecks to make up the campaign contribution kitty. In others, bonuses are inflated by an amount that is expected to be contributed to potential clients.

Not all firms practice this sort of activity, of course, but most successful underwriters do, whether or not they embrace it heartily, reluctantly or are stampeded into it.

New York City Chooses Its Underwriters

We turn again to New York City for an interesting case study of how a municipality chooses its underwriting syndicate. In November 1989, David N. Dinkins was elected the first black mayor of the city. With his comptroller, Elizabeth Holtzman,

Dinkins said he would restructure the city's underwriting syndicate. Minority- and women-owned firms were urged to compete for slots.

The city, always one of the top issuers of debt, said it planned to sell $19 billion for its capital program over the four years until the next election. A spot on this team promised to be very valuable: in 1989, the city paid about $30 million in fees to its underwriters.

Who gave to the successful Dinkins campaign? From Oct. 3 on, when the election campaign was at its height, records show that Goldman, Sachs & Co. gave Dinkins the legal limit of $3,000, while its employees gave another $29,450. First Boston Corp. employees came in second, with $24,000, while Bear, Stearns & Co. employees contributed $19,000. Smith Barney, Harris Upham & Co. ranked fourth, with $18,500, while Kidder, Peabody & Co. bankers chipped in $15,000. Morgan Stanley & Co. bankers gave $14,500, in addition to the firm's own $1,500.

During that same period, employees at Prudential-Bache, Merrill Lynch, Dean Witter Reynolds, Drexel Burnham Lambert, PaineWebber Inc. and Pryor, Govan, Counts & Co. (later renamed Pryor, McClendon, Counts & Co.) also gave around $10,000. Beyond that, the gift-giving was fairly idiosyncratic: Lebenthal & Co. gave $1,000. The "Chemical Bank Fund for Good Government" gave $3,000. Roosevelt & Cross gave $250.

New York City's Questionnaire

The city also sent out a questionnaire to all prospective underwriting firms in the spring of 1990 to see if they fit the city's criteria. The following is a brief review of the survey and an examination of the results both practical and political.

1) Describe your firm's experience and qualifications with respect to: a) senior managing tax-exempt financing of more than $250 million; b) issuers of general obligations; c) New York issues; d) taxable municipal debt; e) variable rate and multi-mode debt; f) zero coupon bonds.

In this section, applicants were asked to describe, in great detail, the amounts and types of tax-exempt issues they had managed in the past, including all the deals they underwrote in New York State, in order to demonstrate their commitment to local financing.

2) What are your specific recommendations as to the frequency, size, structure and type of borrowing that the City should undertake to meet its financing needs?

Applicants were asked to give their views on how the city's volume of debt could best be digested in the open market. They were asked to analyze the need for term bonds and zero coupons to help cash flows, the creation of non-callable serial bonds in low interest periods, and so forth.

3) Describe an innovative financing technique that the City does not currently use and that you would recommend. Quantify the benefits of this financing to the City.

This section provided the public finance people the opportunity to show their stuff. They would describe some esoteric technique or swap program that looks impressive on computer printouts but most likely would never be used.

4) What specific actions do you recommend to the City

to ensure the optimal marketing and placement of its debt? What attributes of your firm would assist the City in the successful marketing of its debt? Please discuss the pre-marketing process, the use of retentions and the appropriate City and managing underwriters' role in the allocation process.

Investment bankers, never known for modesty, were asked to tell the city how their appointment as underwriter would be the best way to market and place the debt. They would describe their distribution capabilities, branch system and the size of their sales forces. Individual applicants would most certainly argue for greater bond retention and a more senior role in the deal.

5) The managing underwriters will be expected to assist the City and its financial advisors in obtaining legislation to reform the New York State Local Finance Law and Federal Law to allow more flexibility in its debt offerings. What specific legislative changes would you recommend and how can your firm assist in this effort?

Because of archaic local finance laws, the applicants could have a field day with this proposal. They would propose greater flexibility in structuring bonds sales and debt service and the ability to sell zero coupon and variable-rate bonds, which the city at that time could not do.

6) Describe your firm's quantitative capabilities, including the ability of your firm to develop specialized software to assist the City in analyzing financing alternatives. Cite specific examples in which you have provided specialized services of this type to other clients.

This was another opportunity for the public finance departments to show their brilliance. They would offer a detailed description of the firm's in-house software and the sorcery it could perform. They listed the firm's computer personnel, their experience and how all this technology would benefit the issuer.

7) Describe your firm's activity and experience in the secondary market generally and specifically for New York City bonds and notes.

The dealer departments supplied this information. They enumerated their average daily inventory and their yearly trading volume. Most of the serious New York dealers employ traders and underwriters dedicated to the New York market. This information would be provided to demonstrate their constant commitment to serving the city.

8) Describe any changes in staffing or staffing policy in the public finance department of your firm in the past three years.

The municipal industry, since 1987, has dramatically contracted due to federal tax reform, the decline in new-issue volume and narrowing profit margins. Salomon Brothers, once the number one underwriter, closed its entire municipal division in 1987 and most other firms have cut personnel. By asking this question, the city was trying to determine if applicants were still seriously involved in the municipal industry.

9) Please provide biographies of the individuals who would constitute your managing underwriting team. Describe only the individuals who would actually work on the City's business. Specify the role each would play as well as what backup coverage would be available in time of conflicting engagements.

10) Provide a list of four relevant governmental units for which your firm acted in the capacity of senior managing underwriter on a negotiated offering within the last three years. Please include the name, title and telephone number of a representative of each issuer familiar with your work in addition to the name of the issue, its rating, and the size and type of issue.

The firms supplied vanity profiles on every senior member of their public finance and dealer departments. References of satisfied clients were also listed.

11) Please describe your firm's commitment to New York City's economy and its residents. Does your firm have any plans to relocate employees into or out of the City in the next three years?

The applicants were asked to describe everything they had ever done in the city. The city was also concerned about the each firm's commitment to maintaining employment within the city's five boroughs.

12) The purpose of this question is to enable the City to determine your firm's business connections, if any, with South Africa. The following information will help the City to formulate an appropriate policy in this area for contracts with underwriters.

Does your firm 1) have agents or employees in South Africa? 2) own property in South Africa? 3) have a contractual arrangement that provides for use of its name, trade name, patents, etc., by any entity doing business in or with South Africa? 4) pay a tax, fee or similar charge to the government of South Africa? 5) participate knowingly in any financial transactions that begin, end or pass through South Africa? 6) do business now or within the past year with the government of South Africa or any corporate or entity controlled by that government;? 7) own or control at least five percent of the voting shares of any entity engaging in activities described in (1) through (6) of this paragraph? (Please state the percentage so owned or controlled.)

13) The City has policies encouraging equal employment opportunity and affirmative action. Please provide the following information: (a) Describe your firm's equal employment opportunity and affirmative action policies and programs. (b) Complete the following form:

The form asked applicants to list the total number of employees, the number and percentage of women, and the number and percentage of minorities, in the governing body (board of directors and executive committee); top management; officers, and all other professionals. This section is self-explanatory. The city wanted to know what kind of affirmative action program the applicant employs.

Who Was Chosen

New York City finally made its selection in mid-June 1989, after a protracted interview period. The results were not very surprising: of the 22 firms selected to the city's syndicate in 1988, 18 were reappointed to the new syndicate. Of the 30 firms finally chosen, six firms owned by minorities or women made the grade.

In the top senior manager slots were Merrill Lynch, Bear, Stearns, First Boston, Goldman Sachs and Shearson Lehman Hutton , all heavyweights in the business.

Named co-managers were BT Securities Corp.; Dillon, Read & Co.; Donaldson, Lufkin & Jenrette Securities Corp.; First Albany Corp.; Grigsby Brandford Powell Inc., a minority-owned firm; Manufacturers Hanover; Morgan Stanley PaineWebber Inc.Prudential-Bache ; Pryor, McClendon, Counts & Co., a minority-owned firm; Samuel A. Ramirez & Co., also a minority-owned firm; Roosevelt & Cross .; Muriel Siebert & Co., which is owned by a woman; Smith Barney, and Dean Witter Reynolds.

A special bracket of 10 firms was named to manage equipment financings. The firms included Artemis Capital Group Inc., which is owned by women; Chemical Securities Inc.; Ehrlich-Bober & Co.; First Chicago Corp.; Kidder, Peabody & Co.; WR Lazard & Laidlaw Inc., a minority-owned firm; Lebenthal & Co.; Marine Midland Capital Markets; J.P. Morgan Securities Inc.; and Tucker Anthony & R.L. Day Inc.

Chapter 7:

Tax-Exempt Financing Techniques: What They Are and Why They Are Used

Beginning in the 1970s, a number of variations on the basic general obligation and revenue bond structures were concocted by issuers and investment bankers, for a variety of reasons.

The benefits to the issuers of such bonds is usually obvious, but their complexity means they must be more carefully explained to investors. Generally speaking, as market resources become stretched — either because long-term interest rates are perceived as too high, or prohibitions are placed on certain kinds of borrowings, or an issuer decides that it just does not want to use up any more of its general obligation bonding capacity — investment bankers and financial advisers become more creative, with the bankers in particular offering numerous products, many of them with catchy names.

Refundings

The simplest type of financing "technique" is the refunding. Usually in such financings, the proceeds of a new bond sale are used to purchase a portfolio of U.S. Treasury securities, whose coupon payments are then used to pay off the remaining debt service on old, refunded bonds until they are called or mature. Such escrowed bonds, called "prerefunded" in the market, are among the safest of all bonds to hold.

From an issuer's point of view, refundings are done to reduce interest costs on earlier bond issues, restructure debt service or eliminate old bond covenants now considered restrictive.

Refundings have been popular with issuers since the market came down from the historic lofty yields of the early 1980s. The biggest year ever for refundings was 1986, when $53.35 billion came to market, accounting for 35% of the $150.99 billion total municipal volume. It has been estimated that about 25% of all municipal bonds outstanding are bonds that have been prerefunded. There are several different kinds of refundings.

A **current refunding** is when the outstanding bonds are called immediately (within 90 days) after the refunding or bought back through tender offers.

An **advance refunding,** or **defeasance,** is when the old bonds are left outstanding until their first call date, which can be years in the future. In advance refundings, which we explained above, proceeds from new "refunding" bonds are used to buy Treasury securities that are put into escrow to pay interest and principal on the old "refunded" bonds as they mature or are called.

A **high-to-low** refunding defeases high-coupon bonds and replaces them with bonds with lower interest rates. A high-to-low refunding, which is larger in size than the refunded issue, is usually done to reduce debt service costs.

A **low-to-high** refunding defeases lower coupon bonds with a smaller number of higher yielding securities. This kind of refunding is often done to eliminate restrictive covenants in the original bond indenture.

A **crossover refunding** occurs when specific revenues are used to pay refunded bonds, and then "cross over" and pay the new refunding bonds when the old bonds are retired.

Synthetic Refunding

Tax reform legislation in the early 1980s specifically prohibited advance refundings for so-called private activity bonds, to prevent two sets of bonds from being issued for the same purpose and two sets of investors from earning tax-exempt income. But investment bankers created some new instruments which allowed issuers to enjoy the benefits of refundings without violating tax law.

The most successful of these came to market in early 1989 under two proprietary names: First Boston Corp.'s refunding escrow deposits, or REDs, and Goldman, Sachs & Co.'s "Municipal Forwards."

Investors who buy REDs or Forwards agree to purchase tax-exempt bonds on a specific date in the future at a particular interest rate. What they are actually doing is buying short-term securities, putting them in escrow, and using the proceeds at maturity to buy refunding bonds on the call date of the original bonds.

The issuer thus gets a chance to lock in current rates, betting that they will move higher in the future. He also gets a chance to stretch project financing into another year in the belief that similar funds might not be available in the future. The investor, for his part, bets that rates will move lower so that his rate of interest is competitive with or better than market rates when he buys the new bonds.

The first REDs issue was done by First Boston for the Omaha Airport Authority on March 21, 1989. The authority sold

$37.655 million of REDs, under which six investors agreed to purchase U.S.Treasury notes in the secondary market, put them in escrow, and use the proceeds when the notes matured on Dec. 31, 1991, to buy the same amount of the authority's refunding bonds. The refunding bonds carried interest rates ranging from 8 1/4% to 8 3/4%. The outstanding bonds, which were sold in 1984 at rates of 10 3/4% to 10 5/8%, were to be retired on Jan. 1, 1992, their first call date. First Boston figured the authority's savings through this refunding to be $500,000 annually through the year 2014.

Not all methods of obtaining relief from prohibitions on advance refundings have succeeded. In early 1990, for example, the Camden County Municipal Utilities Authority in New Jersey sold $236 million in zero coupon capital appreciation bonds to advance refund a portion of a 1987 $242 million sewer bond issue and a separate $192.2 million issue. Because the zeros carry no coupon, the authority has a five-year window during which it is freed from using revenues to make debt service payments on the 1987 bonds.

When the deal first came to light, some market participants criticized it as being similar to abusive "window refundings," proscribed by 1986 tax law, in which taxable debt is used to create a "window "of no debt service, and the freed-up funds are invested in higher-yielding securities to allow the issuer to earn arbitrage profits.

The Camden deal went through. But the Internal Revenue Service in April 1990 said it would move to restrict such deals, while Rep. Beryl Anthony, D-Ark., generally a defender of the market, introduced legislation in Congress designed to prohibit similar deals.

Another method of refinancing that met with some controversy came to market in July 1989, when Shearson Lehman Hutton Inc. essentially securitized two sets of loans for the state of Florida.

The deal worked in this manner: The Florida State Board of Administration "assigned its interest" in loans it had made with earlier bond proceeds to Shearson Lehman, which in turn sold "loan obligations" to investors, who received "custody receipts" to show their ownership of those obligations. Dade County, which received the original loans from the state as part of proceeds from two bond issues totaling $67.5 million done in 1978 and 1983, would continue to make payments on the loans, but now directly to investors, through a custodian bank. Under the terms of the deal, Shearson paid the state $1.35 million more than it needed to deposit into two escrow accounts to defease the bonds.

The issuer made money from an arbitrage play between the yield of the securities it purchased for the escrow accounts and what it got from the investment bank for its loan obligations. Shearson made money by selling the loan obligations to investors for more than it paid to purchase the loan obligations from the issuer. State officials called it "a legally authorized arbitrage game," while certain IRS officials said they thought the deal might be abusive in that it resulted in two sets of securities being outstanding. In any event, the IRS did nothing further about custody receipts, and counsel on the issue said it felt comfortable with the deal's structure.

Municipal Leasing

Municipalities in the late 1970s discovered that their ability to increase their bonded debt was severely hampered. In perhaps the most famous attack on municipal spending authority, on June 6, 1978, California's taxpayers overwhelmingly approved Proposition 13, which slashed property taxes and restricted municipal borrowing. In Massachusetts in 1981, voters approved Proposition 2 1/2, which limited property tax level increases to 2 1/2% of assessed valuation.

To continue meeting the perceived needs of the community, elected officials began employing financing methods that evaded constitutional limitations and the need for voter approval. Municipal leasing became a very popular vehicle because it provided the means for government to own real property, buildings and equipment without selling long-term debt.

A lease, by definition, is an agreement by which a party has the right to use property for a specific time period in return for monetary payment; in other words, rent. When a municipality leases property, the rent becomes a line item in its general operating budget that is re-appropriated every fiscal year.

The three basic lease deals that have been used are:

Straight Operating Lease — The municipality rents property or equipment which is returned when the lease expires. The length of the agreement varies; up to 10 years in the case of equipment, up to 99 years when it involves real property.

Lease-Sublease — In this scenario, the government leases an asset and then sub-leases a portion of it to an outsider who may have no direct relation to the municipal entity. For example, a building is leased to save money, and space that cannot be utilized will be rented to an independent governmental agency or a privately run corporation.

Lease Purchase Agreements — This approach has proven to be the most popular because its structure permits a municipality to own the leased property, and without issuing bonds.

When a municipality signs a lease purchase agreement for a certain period of time, it agrees to make installment payments based on the market value of the asset. This procedure has permitted municipalities to obtain new school buildings, computer and telephone systems, garbage and fire trucks, police cars and medical equipment and to renovate buildings and stadiums. In 1980, less than $500 million in lease-backed debt was sold. Today, 38 states allow it, and in 1989 over $6 billion in leases were issued.

It is possible to underwrite lease purchase agreements and sell them to individual and institutional investors. The interest portion of the monthly lease payment is tax-exempt, just like municipal bonds. This tax-exemption exists only with lease purchase agreements because for the interest to be tax-free, the municipality must acquire ownership of the property when the lease is terminated.

Most of the time, these deals are structured for distribution as certificates of participation. When an investor purchases a COP, he owns a piece of the lease and is entitled to a share of the municipality's lease payments.

The major risk for a shareholder is the failure of the municipality to appropriate money to fund the lease. Funding must be approved every fiscal year, and in lean times, as with all appropriations, politicians might look to cut payments to leased projects.

To minimize investment risks, investors should make sure the indenture contains a non-substitution clause. This prevents the municipality from breaking an equipment lease in order to substitute similar equipment manufactured by a competing firm. In an age of constantly improving telephone and computer systems, this protection clause is essential.

Master leases have been created as another protection against non-appropriation. This contract covers, in one stroke, various types of equipment (for example, telephones, computers and typewriters) deemed essential for the day to day operation of a given political sub-division. Since the indenture does not permit the municipality to selectively refuse to appropriate funds for a given piece of equipment, it is unlikely that the entire contract would be voided to alter only one of the systems.

Lease-backed certificates of participation have defaulted, but not many. In 1990, for example, a deal defaulted when a Florida circuit court judge declared that the state legislature could void a lease on a $15 million research and development complex called Innovation Park. Investors should be leery of COPs like this because studies have shown that most defaulted leases involve highly speculative technology that is of marginal importance to a municipality.

Zero Coupon Bonds

Even though zero coupon bonds do not pay any interest until maturity and have the most price volatility of any tax-exempt security, they are still one of the most popular investment vehicles. Why so? Because they are sold at a very deep discount, they appeal to those who want to own tax-exempt bonds but do not have the cash available to buy current coupon bonds.

In addition, those investors who do not need to draw down any income from their investments find zeros to be a painless method to build an estate or to prepare for future college costs. Several states, in fact, have specifically targeted such investors for "college savers" programs. Finally, the shrewd investor views zeros as a way to avoid the re-investment risk inherent in conventional tax-exempt securities.

In the early 1980s, when interest rates hit record highs, investors were anxious to purchase zero coupon bonds when they thought rates hit the top of the market. They were even willing to accept less yield — 10 1/2% for 30-year zeros vs. 11% for 30-year current coupon bonds — because they knew they were locking in high yields and did not have to face the risk of future coupon income re-investments at possibly very low yields.

Many investors profited handsomely with zeros purchased in 1981-1982. But there are potential risks and negatives to buying zero coupon bonds.

1. As a result of the guaranteed re-investment rate, traders view zeros as the most volatile of securities. The general rule is that their value will move up or down three times faster than traditional coupon bonds. So, if the investor calls rates incorrectly, he may witness a rapid decline in principal.

2. Call features of zeros can work against the investor. It makes no sense to accept less yield if the issuer can call bonds in a declining rate environment.

3. The creditworthiness of the issuer is vital. Since zeros pay no money until maturity, if the issuer goes bust, the investor, after sitting on the bonds for years, will have nothing to show for his efforts.

A variation of the zero coupon bond is the Compound Interest Bond or "Municipal Multiplier." This bond is issued at par with a coupon, but the interest payments are not released until maturity. Like zeros, the interest payments are reinvested at the bond's coupon level.

For the municipality, there is little real downside to issuing zeros. Not having to pay out any money until maturity is very attractive, as is the savings on administrative costs.

Such securities, highly prized by investors, rarely trade in the market, and those issuers that decide to issue a few zero-coupon maturities quickly find such maturities oversubscribed. Salesmen find them a natural sell to investors, once properly explained.

Bond Banks

State bond banks buy smaller bond issues from localities and then sell larger offerings. This arrangement cuts borrowing costs for the local issuers because the bond banks' debt usually carries higher ratings than municipalities can command, most often because state bond bank debt is backed by the state's moral obligation.

Bond banks have many advantages, for all parties to the transaction. Tiny, often unrated issuers enjoy the economies of scale and are able to tap the credit markets rather than having to borrow from commercial banks, which is more expensive. The bond bank, because of the implicit state guarantee, is able to get the municipalities lower interest rates, and may even purchase some forms of credit enhancement, such as bond insurance, to ensure even lower rates. Underwriters and salesmen need not delve into the creditworthiness of each locality participating in a bond bank issue, but simply operate with the bond bank's state name. Investors, for their part, rely on the security the state's name lends to the issuers.

Bond banks have operated in Canadian provinces since the 1940s. Vermont established the first state bond bank in 1969. Maine, Alaska, North Dakota, New Hampshire, New York, Illinois, Indiana, the city of Indianapolis and Puerto Rico all have functioning bond banks.

Pooled Financings

Pooled financings were developed as an effective means of raising money for many projects at one time. The reasoning behind the development of pools was pretty much the same as the idea behind bond banks — a number of participants could gain access to the tax-exempt market and take advantage of the economies of scale.

In the mid-1980s, a number of so-called "blind pools" were sold in which issuers rushed deals to market to take advantage of lower interest rates or proposed unfavorable tax legislation, without actually having specific projects in mind. Proceeds from such issues were often invested to earn arbitrage profits; many of them were also later "collapsed" or refunded, the proceeds unspent, the benefits of tax-exemption going to the issuers in the form of arbitrage, and to bankers and lawyers in the form of fees. Both Congress and the IRS subsequently specifically prohibited the issuance of blind pools, and the IRS is known to be looking at a number of the ones that came to market to determine if they were abusive.

Tax-Increment Bonds

In general, tax increment bonds are issued by redevelopment agencies as part of a financing program to eliminate urban blight or to ease the way for development. The tax increment concept derives its name from the increases in property taxes generated by such development. These taxes help to pay off the bonds as well as fund other improvements. More than half of the states currently allow tax increment financing.

A redevelopment tax-increment financing begins by calculating the base amount of tax assessments within an urban renewal area before implementation of the renewal plan. Any subsequent tax revenue increases over this base amount are assumed to be by-products of the redevelopment efforts, and the urban renewal authority may use these incremental taxes to repay bonds or fund other improvements.

California issuers in particular have embraced the concept of tax-increment financing, primarily because of the Proposition 13 limits on property tax increases and GO bond issuance. Act 1911 and 1915 Special Assessment Bonds, Mello-Roos bonds and tax-allocation bonds are all sold by special districts to fund development and are substitutes for property-tax backed GOs. All but the tax allocation bonds are usually unrated, with the investment riskiness that connotes.

During periods of economic slowdown, the risks of tax-increment financing become readily apparent. Simply put, if there is no growth or development within the jurisdiction that sold the bonds, there will not be sufficient increases in tax revenues to repay the debt. This was demonstrated in dramatic fashion in Colorado in the early 1990s when a number of issuers, which sold tax-increment debt counting on the real estate boom going on indefinitely, faced default when the real estate market swooned.

Standard & Poor's, in an October 1990 report on tax increment debt, reported that such debt is vulnerable to economic conditions, changes in tax rates and legislation exempting certain kinds of property from taxation. Moreover, the agency noted, "These projects are sold as things that will "pay for themselves,' which may mean other taxing entities are reluctant to step in if things go wrong." Investors should realize that tax increment debt may offer handsome yields, but is speculative by its very nature.

Warrants

A tax-exempt warrant, attached to a municipal bond , guarantees the owner the right to purchase like bonds in the future at the same price and yield as the bond presently held. The warrant, which is redeemable to the bearer and can be clipped from the bond and sold, is good for two years. Financiers view it as a reverse tender option because the owner, when exercising the option, has the power to direct the municipality to issue more debt.

During anticipated high interest rate periods, warrants are popular with municipalities. The issuer is betting that interest rates will be higher in two years and that the warrants will expire without being exercised. If it wins the bet, the municipality saves money over the life of the issue because the investor, by accepting the warrant, settles for a yield on the original issue below prevailing rates.

Let's look at an example: If a 30-year bond commands a yield of 10%, the investor would accept 9 1/4% for the same maturity if a warrant is attached. During the life of the warrant, if rates for 30-year bonds drop to 8%, the owner will exercise the warrant and get additional bonds that pay 9 1/4%. In this scenario, the municipality loses the bet and must pay an extra 1 1/4% interest for 30 years.

The first warrants were issued in February 1981 by New York's Municipal Assistance Corporation (MAC). It sold several series of bonds with warrants, including $59 million 12 3/4% bonds. By the time those warrants expired, rates had dropped to 11%, and the additional debt MAC had to take on is now costing New Yorkers an additional $1 million a year in debt service payments.

In addition to the risks involved, municipalities have also learned that warrants can create a bureaucratic mess. Each time a warrant is exercised (the indenture sets aside one day a month for redemptions), the issuer must update its disclosure statements as if a new bond is created. With the general decline in rates during the latter part of the 1980s, warrants were rarely used in the new-issue market.

Variable-Rate Securities and Other Devices

Tax-exempt portfolio managers will always view the early 1980s as the "Nightmare Years." Spiralling inflation caused dramatic interest rate increases and incredible market volatility. On May 8, 1980, the *Bond Buyer's* index of 20-year municipal bonds stood at 7.11%; by Jan. 14, 1982, that figure had jumped to an all-time high of 13.14%, with a corresponding drop in bond prices. Little wonder why money managers were numb.

During this same period, the popularity of short-term tax-exempt money market funds soared. Individuals reacting to devastating market conditions wanted instant liquidity, and municipal money market funds met their demands.

To service these gun-shy retail investors, public finance investment banking departments created investment vehicles that attempted to preserve capital and at the same time provide liquidity. The techniques described in the remainder of this chapter are the products that evolved during this era.

Variable Rate Debt

Variable or Floating Rate Securities have maturities as long as 30 years, but there is a feature that permits the yield to be adjusted on a daily, weekly or monthly basis. The yields are based on an index tied to a fixed percentage of the prime rate, the Treasury bill rate or even the Bond Buyer Index. In addition, the owner has the right to give notice, before each adjustment date, that he intends to give back the securities to the issuer and get his money back.

To insure liquidity and necessary cash flow to the issuer, variable rate securities are backed by a bank back-up facility in the form of a line of credit or letter of credit.

A line of credit is designed to lend an issuer funds, when needed, for a certain period of time in order to meet redemptions. If, on a yield readjustment date, the issuer is hit with several million dollars worth of redemptions and does not have enough cash on hand, it can draw on the line of credit to meet the shortfall. One must be aware, however, that the bank's obligations are limited: the line of credit is null and void if the issuer goes into default. The cost for this bank service is negotiable and can range annually from 10 basis points, or one-tenth of 1%, to 50 basis points of the deal's size.

A letter of credit is an irrevocable guarantee by a bank to pay the principal and interest payments of an issuer. It is another means to insure adequate cash flow and sometimes it is valid even if the issuer goes into default. The letter of credit can also enhance the municipality's rating because investors look to the bank, not the municipality, for ultimate repayment. Municipal bond insurance and letters of credit are similar because both relieve the investor of credit risk. They differ in that letters of credit charge yearly fees and do not necessarily limit the size of the guarantee.

Floating rate securities are very popular with tax-exempt money market funds because the SEC has ruled that the readjustment date can be treated as the maturity date — not the 20- or 30-year actual maturity. So in addition to being guaranteed current market yields, the fund manager can maintain the portfolio's required short average life.

A modified version of the variable rate concept is the flexible rate note. These notes are issued with a fixed coupon rate and often have maturities of 30, 60 or 90 days. At the end of the stated time period, there is in effect a mandatory put, and the owner has the option to repurchase the notes at a new rate. This rate, however, is not tied to an index. The underwriter announces a yield based on its perception of market conditions.

A variation of the variable rate bond structure appeared in early 1990. Shearson Lehman Hutton unveiled what it called RIBs and SAVRs, its service marks for "residual interest bonds" and "select auction variable rate securities."

The structure made its debut in a negotiated $120 million issue for the Nebraska Investment Finance Authority. The deal comprised $50 million in SAVRs, $50 million in RIBs, and $20 million of bonds to refund some earlier bonds.

The deal worked this way: Both portions of the loan came due in 2022. The SAVRs portion of the deal had a variable interest rate set at Dutch auction every 35 days at which investors stipulate the lowest rate they will accept. The initial rate was set at 6%.

The other half of the issue, the RIBs, had a rate determined by the difference between the 7.666% payment stream made by the issuer and the variable interest rate paid on the SAVRs. In other words, the authority's debt service was capped at $7.66 million per year on the $100 million RIBs and SAVRs. If at the next Dutch auction the rate paid on the SAVRs was 6%, about $3 million of debt service would go toward paying SAVRs holders. The remaining $4.66 million was divided among holders of the $50 million RIBs. At the first sale, that translated to an 8.89% yield.

Thus, every five weeks, the debt service payments by the issuer will be divided up. The lower the short-term SAVRs sell for at auction, the higher the RIBs' interest rates will go; the cost to the issuer does not change. If short-term rates sky-rocket, of course, there is the potential for a RIBs' holder to receive no payment. Bankers interviewed at the time predicted that if rates looked like they were about to soar, an investor could always buy a SAVR, and in essence get the equivalent of a fixed-rate bond.

Bankers who worked on the deal said this particular issue saved the authority 21 basis points: the normal net interest cost would have been 7.875%, but the new structure enabled the authority to bring that down to 7.666%, which meant a $6.3 million savings on the $100 million deal.

Variable rate bonds, born of the volatile, high interest rate environment of the 1980s, have been used in a number of combinations, with taxable bonds, with fixed-rate bonds, and with a variety of conversion features allowing their issuers to lock in fixed rates. The basic structure, however, is the same.

Put Bonds

The technical name of this product is option tender bonds. Traders, however, refer to them as "puts" because the owner of the security can "put" them back to the issuer at the original cost and at a time period prior to the stated maturity of the bonds. The idea is to limit exposure by giving the owner the choice, based on his market perspective, to convert his long-term bonds into a short-term investment.

A typical putable bond deal is structured to have a term bond with a maturity of 20 to 30 years. Attached to the bond is an option in which the holder can tender the bonds back to the issuer and receive par on a specific date. It can be a one-year put, but most of the time puts can be exercised in three to five years after the issue date.

The yield in this type of deal is about 100 basis points less than a normal 20- or 30- year term bond. Nevertheless, the put bond is still attractive because it yields around 100 basis points more than a similar conventional bond that matures at the same time the tender option can be exercised. In other words, the investor owns a piece of paper that outperforms short-term investments, but if the market undergoes a dramatic decline in rates, he has the opportunity to lock in an attractive rate by not exercising the put.

For the issuer, there are major advantages. He has an easier time raising capital and saves 75 to 125 basis points on the cost of borrowing. But he does have one major obligation to ensure marketability and liquidity: he must have available a backup facility that provides the funds necessary to cover exercised puts. This is essential because in high interest-rate environments, bondholders could flood the issuer with redemptions. Once again, it should be remembered that a line of credit only provides liquidity for exercised puts. All deals are off if the issuer goes into default.

Put deals also have call dates. If there is a major decline in interest rates, even though the put is not exercised, the owner can lose his bonds if the issuer decides to call them.

Tax-Exempt Commercial Paper

Tax-exempt commercial paper is a popular technique to help meet seasonal borrowing needs on ongoing capital spending programs. Similar in concept to corporate commercial paper, it is a short-term temporary unsecured note backed by a bank letter or line of credit. The paper's life extends from one to 270 days and is rolled over until permanent financing is issued.

Tax-exempt commercial paper first appeared in December 1972 in a pollution control deal for Virginia Electric Power Co., which also contained a revolving bank credit agreement.

The ultimate credit support for commercial paper is the pledged revenues of the given project or the general obligation pledge of the municipality. A line of credit provides liquidity and is not a substitute for creditworthiness. Pledging the general obligation of a governmental entity is the usual condition banks demand before agreeing to a backup facility. Under this arrangement, if the issuer draws down on the credit line, the bank can legally force the issuer to raise property taxes in order to secure money owned.

From the issuer's standpoint, tax-exempt commercial paper is viewed as an investment vehicle that is superior to bond anticipation notes because it is not issued for a fixed time. In New York State, for instance, BANs must have a specific maturity date and can be rolled over only a certain number of times. Also, tax-exempt commercial paper furnishes an issuer with greater flexibility and a lower net borrowing cost. There are several factors that must be considered and analyzed by the issuer before determining whether or not the initiation of a commercial paper program makes sense:

1. Administrative overhead can be costly because commercial paper requires daily attention. Many municipalities pondering such programs often fail to take this into consideration.

2. Commercial paper bond counsel fees, letter of credit fees and underwriting fees are more expensive than conventional financing.

3. Unlike bond, revenue and tax anticipation notes, which can be underwritten on short notice, a commercial paper program can take several months to organize.

4. The rating agencies demand greater disclosure. Quarterly or monthly financial data must be supplied.

Tender Option Programs

Another vehicle created in the early 1980s to help solve the liquidity problems of bank portfolio managers was the Tender Option Program, a service mark of Merritt Forbes & Co.

The big increase in interest rates caused the market value of bank investment portfolios to drop significantly. And even though the banks' need for tax-exempt income declined due to poor earnings, they were in no great rush to sell their municipal holdings because they would have to incur additional losses. Regulatory approved accounting practices permit banks to keep municipal holdings at original cost; only when they actually sell a security must it be marked to a market price. Hence, a bank can hold on its books at 100 cents on the dollar a bond with a 2% coupon even though the bond might only be worth 40 cents on the open market.

The tender option program was developed to permit banks to unload their low coupon bonds without taking the entire loss. This is possible because the bonds are sold with a put option attached in which the new owner can, at some future time, sell back the bonds to the bank at a fixed "strike price."

A letter of credit guarantees that money will be available if the put is exercised. (The LOC is terminated, however, if the TOP bond is called or if the municipality goes into default.) To make the TOPs offering more attractive than current offerings, a strike price is assigned that results in a yield higher than the present market commands. For example, if a 5% bond maturing in 2010 is worth a dollar price of 55, the same 5% security may be worth 75 if it matured in two years. To make the TOPs bond a better purchase than a regular two-year bond, the strike price would be 77. This would yield several basis points above the market for a new two-year municipal bond.

The put is a one-time affair, and if the new owner misses it, he owns the bonds based on their original maturity. If rates experience a big drop prior to the put date, the owner may keep the bonds because the long-term maturity yield is now a value. An increase in yields may cause the investor to put back the bonds in order to invest the proceeds at higher levels.

For TOPs to work, there must be a tremendous demand for short-term paper and taxable rates must be substantially higher than municipal yields.

What are the advantages of employing this technique? The buyer of the TOPs gets attractive tax-exempt yields for a short period; the seller (who really doesn't need tax-exempt income) reinvests the proceeds in taxable securities and makes significantly higher income.

Municipal Bond Swaps

Swaps are not a financing technique as such, but can be done in the primary market to save an issuer money. The parties involved in such deals, which are fairly new to the municipal bond market but old-hat to the corporate bond market, where they originated in the 1980s, essentially "trade" interest rate payment terms. The issuer works out the terms of the deal with brokerage house or bank to swap its fixed interest payments for floating rates, or vice versa.

Philadelphia was the first major city to complete a municipal interest rate swap transaction in 1990, when it sold $148 million GO variable-rate debt and swapped the bonds to a fixed rate after the sale.

Such transactions are rife with risk, and are now done with about 5% to 10% of the new-issue market. Issuers should not attempt them without the services of a financial adviser.

Bond Insurance

New York City's financial collapse and the WPPSS debacle both served to jar the nerves of retail investors. To calm those nerves, underwriters turned to municipal bond insurance.

When an underwriter purchases insurance for a particular deal, the company providing the coverage guarantees to pay principal and interest if the issuer fails to pay on a due date.

At the time of the underwriting of a new issue (insurers also are active in the secondary market, often insuring all or parts of municipal bond portfolios), the following events usually take place:

Shortly before the pricing meeting, the manager of the underwriting syndicate will call the leading insurers and ask what they would charge to insure the bonds for the life of the issue. The insurance companies have already had their research analysts examine the municipality and have determined if they wish to cover it. If they are so inclined, they will quote a fee, usually ranging from 1/2% to 3% of the face value of the issue. Since the underwriter is talking to carriers who are all rated triple-A by either or both Moody's and Standard and Poor's, he makes his choice based on which company will charge the lowest price.

At the syndicate meeting, the underwriters structure the deal using both insured and uninsured bonds and will go with the scenario in which they can sell the most bonds. Sometimes, part of a deal is insured while the remainder is uninsured. This is often done to accommodate a potential buyer.

Municipalities of low investment quality (Baa/BBB) do not object to paying the fees because they know that in the long run they will make back the cost of the insurance several times in lower borrowing costs.

Bond insurance also makes the bond salesman's job much easier. Rather than taking the time to describe an obscure credit or a complex financing structure, he can simply tell the potential investor that the bond is insured. Investors, for their part, consider bond insurance "sleep insurance."

Birth of the Industry

Municipal bond insurance had been discussed as early as April 1897, when *The Daily Bond Buyer* reported on the novel concept of "Municipal Bond Insurance." The front page story outlined the "considerable interest excited among bond dealers and investors" by the "First Municipal Bond Assurance Company of America," organized in 1895. The firm intended to insure municipal bonds both in the primary and secondary markets and in portfolios, guaranteeing both principal and interest payments. But the writer at the time called the proposal "problematical." He noted, "The first class Cities which are selling low rate interest bearing bonds for long terms at a high basis just now, are not likely to ask any insurance for which they will have to pay. It is uncertain as yet if any large purchaser or original issues of bonds by large cities will be willing to pay any considerable percentage to have guaranteed the bonds which the cities themselves guarantee." The firm, perhaps the result of low spreads — yields at the time ranged around 3% — vanished without a trace.

It is generally agreed that the modern bond insurance industry was born in 1971, when Gerald L. Friedman of MGIC and Frank Carr, formerly president of John Nuveen & Co., founded American Municipal Bond Assurance Corp. as a subsidiary of MGIC.

By 1973, more than $1 million in par value of new-issue bonds had been insured by AMBAC. The amount grew steadily. Insured total volume hit $1.15 billion in 1977, $1.16 billion in 1980, $2.34 billion in 1981, $6.76 billion in 1982, $12.81 billion in 1983, and $16.18 billion in 1984. In 1985, insured volume hit a record $44.39 billion, or over 20% of the total $205 billion in long-term debt sold.

The growth of the insurance business closely paralleled the increase in individual investors, as opposed to institutions, in the marketplace. Individuals, now the dominant buyers of municipal bonds, do not want to hear about risk when talking about what is often their retirement money. Retail investors are usually risk averse, and often will sacrifice a few basis points in yield in exchange for the added security of bond insurance.

Friedman in 1986 described the founding of the industry: "When Frank Carr and I founded the industry, we felt that the premium level had to anticipate losses in excess of [those incurred during] the Depression, because municipal bonds, primarily general obligation then, are being used for different purposes these days. So I tried to structure a premium level which would allow for a claims tolerance of between six and 12 [defaults] per 100 issues.

"In other words, for every 100 issues you and I might originate today, the premium, and the investment income thereon, would have to tolerate six to 12 defaults in order to pass my own tests. Of course, whether it's six or 12 depends on whether it's a GO issue or a hospital issue, and what the profile of a loss would be. We try to do loss profiles on every type of issue" to determine the premium.

On average, he noted, "the profile would run something like this: On a bond with a 20-year duration, no defaults for five years, presumably a good underwriting effort, but a total default in years six and seven. Finally, in years eight through 20, payments equaling 75% of debt service. Based on that kind of a loss profile, a front-end premium of about 0.80% on principal and interest would allow a company to tolerate a loss of six to 12 per 100" issues. Premiums in the business generally range from 0.5% to 1.5%.

Two major factors determine premium levels. The first is competition. The more insurers there are, the more price-cutting there will be. Such price cutting was visited upon the market with a vengeance in 1986 and 1987, as new-issue volume contracted and insurers fought to retain market share.

The second factor affecting spread is quality. When the difference between an A-rated bond and a triple-A becomes so narrow that the cost of the insurance premium eats up the enhanced value, there is less need for insurance. Consequently, insurers, scrambling for new issues to guarantee, cut their premiums.

The Industry Booms

The bond insurance industry grew enormously following its founding, and especially throughout the 1980s. In 1974, the Municipal Bond Insurance Association a consortium of five general insurers, was formed. MBIA dominated the business during the 1980s. In December 1986, four of the original five members of the association put up $427.7 million in capital to create MBIA Corp., a so-called "monoline" insurer, monoline meaning that the firm had only one line of business: financial guaranties. The company then went public in 1987. Bond Investors Guaranty Insurance Co. founded at the end of 1985, was purchased in 1989 by MBIA.

Friedman's own Financial Guaranty Insurance Co. was formed in 1983. FGIC went public in 1986, then was purchased by GE Capital in 1988. AMBAC itself was acquired in 1985 by Citibank, which in 1991 sold more than half of its stake in the company to the public through an initial public offering of stock.

Capital Guaranty Insurance Co. was founded at the end of 1986, assuming the book of business of United States Fidelity & Guaranty Insurance Co. And Financial Security Assurance Co., founded in September 1985 as a corporate bond insurer by some veteran municipal bond experts, not long after entered the primary municipal bond market.

The industry has not been without its share of controversy. Shortly after FGIC's founding, Friedman became an outspoken critic of the way bond insurance business was being done. As early as 1986, he decried the practice of premium cutting in order to win business, and in May 1987 blasted his fellow insurers for "compromising their balance sheets to write business."

Insured bonds are not always necessarily triple-A, as some investors have found to their chagrin. In January 1986, Standard & Poor's downgraded to AA 267 issues totaling $5.2 billion insured by Industrial Indemnity Co., a unit of Crum and Forster Inc., because of the insurer's financial difficulties.

The rating agency later downgraded United States Fidelity & Guaranty, to AA from AAA,   affecting 73 issues totaling $1.1 billion. Capital Guaranty subsequently picked up most of the USF&G book, and the bonds returned to a Standard & Poor's AAA.

The bond insurance world also contains a number of smaller insurers and reinsurers, which reinsure bond issues that the primary insurers want to move off of their books.

When it comes to trading, insured bonds take on a world of their own. They do not trade the same as bonds that are rated triple- A on their own merit; generally there is a basis point difference. Bond traders do not treat insured bonds equally. Many look at the underlying rating of the municipality and then assign various value.

In the case of a default, the insurance company will honor the payment of principal and interest to bondholders after the appropriate bonds or coupons are turned over to it. The insurance company becomes the owner of the redeemed bonds and it is the insurer's responsibility to begin legal actions to recover the defaulted payments. The insurers all have extensive surveillance efforts, and usually head off default well in advance through a variety of administrative and financial actions.

Chapter 8:

Investors: Who They Are, What They Buy, and Why

The rise of the individual, or retail buyer, as the dominant force in the municipal bond market was one of the top stories of the 1980s. According to data contained in the Federal Reserve Board's *Flow of Funds Accounts*, which charts who holds municipal bonds and other kinds of debt, households in 1990 held $286.2 billion of the almost $800 billion in tax-exempt debt outstanding — almost double that of the next largest holder, property and casualty insurance companies, which owned $155.5 billion. Commercial banks came in next, with $132.9 billion.

Households had been big holders of municipals all during the decade. But the big change came in 1987.

Before that, banks could deduct 80% of the interest costs they incurred to carry their tax-exempt investment portfolios. The Tax Reform Act of 1986 largely eliminated that deduction, retaining it only for debt purchased from issuers who expect to sell less than $10 million in bonds annually. Issuers hope that the limit will be raised to $25 million, but until it is, banks will buy municipals sparingly.

A Myth Demolished

A common criticism of tax-exempt bonds is that they are owned almost entirely by The Rich. Yet a look at the figures shows that this is not so. The latest Internal Revenue Service statistics show that low- and middle-income taxpayers — those with adjusted gross incomes of $100,000 or less — held half of the $34.6 billion of tax-exempt interest that was reported for 1988, even after the bulk of wealthy taxpayers' returns were taken into account.

Naturally, members of the bond community were delighted by such reports. "It just confirms the fact that ownership in tax-exempt bonds is representative of a cross section of income levels," said Micah Green, executive vice president of the PSA. Cathy Spain, director of the Government Finance Officers Association's federal liaison center, noted, "Isn't this exactly what we've been saying in the past? Now that the tax-exempt bond market is more accessible to individuals through mutual funds and unit trusts," a broader range of taxpayers is purchasing them, she said.

The rise of retail buyers has had a number of immediate effects:

Holders of Municipal Debt: 1946-91

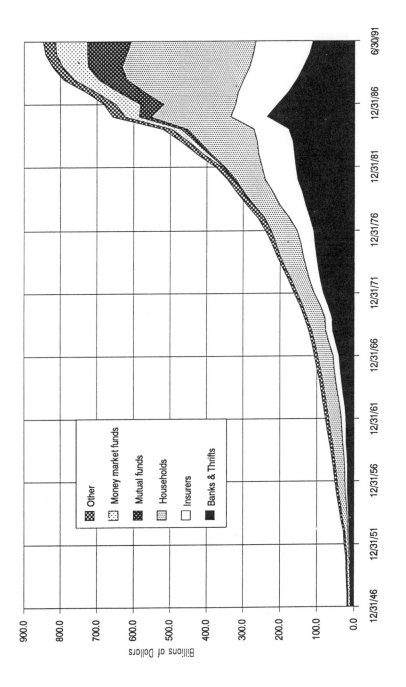

1. The use of municipal bond insurance has exploded. Today, about 25% of the market is routinely enhanced by one of the major bond insurers, who offer, as they have said in the past, "sleep insurance." Retail investors are willing to sacrifice a few basis points in yield in return for having principal and interest payments guaranteed. And salesmen readily acknowledge how much easier it is to sell generic triple-A rated paper, where the sales pitch can rely on the insurer's triple-A rating, not a detailed discussion of the components of the deal.

Institutional investors, on the other hand, rarely buy insured paper because they are hungry for yield and have their own analytical staffs to assess the creditworthiness of bonds.

2. Trading has declined. Retail buyers, in general, unlike institutions, buy bonds to hold, not to trade on incremental moves in price.

3. Municipal research and marketing departments have expanded, and risen in importance, as sales staffs look for ways to describe complicated credits to their retail customers.

Why Retail Investors Buy Municipal Bonds

The primary draw to municipal bonds is their tax-exempt status, as well as their security. The difference between tax-exempt and taxable yields varies as income and tax rates rise. In the lowest tax bracket — for those couples with a taxable income below $30,950, or single households with a taxable income below $18,550 — to equal a tax-exempt yield of 6%, the investor would have to make 7.06% on a taxable investment.

An investor in the 28% tax bracket would have to make 8.33% to match his 6% tax-exempt yield, while an investor in the top tax bracket — 33% — would have to make 8.96% on his taxable investment. The advantages to tax-exempt bonds, then, are obvious.

Tax-exempt bonds, while free of most kinds of federal taxation, are subject to a variety of state taxes, including income, property and capital gains taxes. At least 35 states tax out-of-state bonds, offering investors in in-state bonds a decided advantage — up to 100 basis points or more, according to Gabriele, Hueglin & Cashman's *Guide to State and Local Taxation of Municipal Bonds* (1981).

What They Buy

Individual investors buy everything: actual bonds, unit investment trusts, closed- and open-end mutual funds, and even tax-exempt money market funds, depending on how much money they have and the size of their portfolios.

One of the most popular investments for individual investors today are so-called college saving zero-coupon bonds. Sold at deep discounts, they pay no current interest but are repaid at maturity at full value. It is comparatively easy, then, to structure a portfolio of quality, noncallable paper to mature exactly as one's children are entering college, or when one expects to retire.

In recent years there has been an explosion in the number of books purporting to tell investors how to buy tax-free bonds and not get burned. There has even been one guide, written by a former broker and aimed at registered representatives, on *How to Sell Tax-Free Bonds.* There are certain advantages to all of these books, which for the most part rely on investor common sense.

There are a few fundamentals to be learned, however, whether one is on the buy or the sell side. Perhaps Steven P. Rappaport best summed up the situation in his 1990 book, *The Affluent Investor: Investment Strategies for All Markets.* In his guide, Rappaport said the product must always fit the customer. In other words, there is no good stock or good bond; the customer makes it so.

"The investment process is stood on its head and rightly so," he wrote. "It is not whether the stock market is going up so that certain stocks may be appropriate investments, or even if interest rates are expected to move downward so that the bond portion of the portfolio should be lengthened and funds should be invested in bonds of longer maturities. The first step is, in fact, the analysis of the investment climate and the expected one, *but it must then be evaluated from the point of view of an individual investor,* as one of a group" [italics ours].

This means simply that the affluent investor, or the one with a portfolio of about $50,000 or more, has a different pain threshold than the investor who has a portfolio of $5,000. The larger investor can ride out market volatility more easily.

Fundamentals

The first thing an investor, and the salesman who wants to keep him as a customer, should learn is not to reach for yield. An Arkansas nursing home bond with a 13% yield may be very attractive if yield is one's only measure of beauty. That 13% yield palls rather quickly, however, if the bond goes into default and is not paid, and the workout brings the bondholder only 20 cents on the dollar. More investors get caught in this yield trap every year than in any other way.

The question of reaching for yield aside, the customer should understand something of the nature of the market: why certain bonds sell at a premium; why certain bonds are insured and how many basis points in yield he might lose because they are insured; why certain bonds sell at a discount; and the nature of early redemption features. He should also understand what mutual funds do, if he decides to buy shares in one, and why the middle-man nature of funds typically take away about six points in value from the bonds he "buys."

The wise investor should also realize that the tax-exempt bond market is an over-the-counter one, where pricing is often subjective, and where quotes on the majority of issues could be as much as a few points apart, depending on the dealer. There has been talk in recent years of somehow making pricing more uniform, but the size and diversity of the market make this seem unlikely.

It is little wonder that the complexity of the market makes many salesmen simply put their clients into the comparative safety and homogeneity of unit investment trusts or tax-exempt money market fund.

The Institutions

Retail customers may be the largest holder of tax-exempts, but the bread and butter clients of salesmen and traders are large institutional investors, who place big buy and sell orders and regularly change the composition of their portfolios. There are almost 2,000 property and casualty insurance companies, and they hold approximately $152 billion in tax-exempt debt.

The Investment Company Institute in 1990 reported that 17 major sponsors run a total of 10,475 tax-exempt unit investment trusts, with a total market value of $92.27 billion. This includes every permutation of UIT — fixed-rate, floating-rate, single state, national and high-yield.

There are over 500 tax-exempt mutual funds, with net assets of about $100 billion, and more than 200 money market funds, with assets of over $70 billion. The largest funds, naturally enough, are those of high-tax states — California, with around $21 billion, and New York, with about $11 billion.

But while UITs and mutual funds are surely institutional investors, they are really proxies for retail customers.

Chapter 9:

The Regulators

The municipal bond market is subject to a number of regulators, many of whose interest in the market waxes and wanes depending on the amount of perceived abuses said to be going on in it, and the need for revenues.

During the 1980s, the market saw itself inundated by political and juridical regulation. At the most basic level, various aspects of the market were regulated by states, cities and even individual issuers. States, for one, determine how out of state bonds will be taxed, if they are taxed at all. Cities have put into place rules governing whether bond counsel will be paid on a fee, or an hourly, basis. Issuers, from authorities to states, have enacted laws governing everything from minority underwriter participation in bond deals to how bonds will be distributed.

The market is regulated by Congress and its various tax-writing committees, by the Supreme Court, as well as state and federal courts. It is regulated by actual governmental regulatory bodies, quasi-governmental operations and by trade groups.

Bond Counsel

The market's first level of "regulation," albeit at a most unofficial level, is squarely with the bond counsel. The National Association of Bond Lawyers in its 1988 handbook, *Selection and Evaluation of Bond Counsel*, clearly states, "The purpose of the bond opinion is to provide assurance to investors. It removes from the pricing of bonds the risk of invalidity, lack of enforceability, or interest being includable in gross income for federal income tax purposes. This result can be achieved only if bond counsel's opinion is accepted as reliable in the bond market."

The bond counsel ensure, or are supposed to ensure, that tax-exempt bond issues comply with the letter of tax law. They rule that a certain bond issue is tax-exempt, and will remain so. The bond counsel are, in a sense, in the last trench.

Yet during the late 1980s this changed, because the abuses in the tax-exempt market that sparked the interest of congressmen and their tax aides, the IRS and the SEC, were not done by little-known developers for obscure projects through private placements and by boiler-room bankers. Rather, the deals that aroused the ire of Congress and the rest were most often well-crafted gambles to beat arbitrage prohibitions —

deals "close enough to the edge, and perhaps even beyond," in the words of one bond lawyer — that were approved and in some cases perhaps driven by the very professionals designed to uphold the law.

Joseph Johnson, a partner in the Birmingham, Ala., law firm of Johnson & Thorington, upon stepping down as president of the National Association of Bond Lawyers in 1989, decried this state of affairs, in particular "opinion shopping," in which investment banking firms and financial advisers pressured bond counsel to give a favorable opinion on an issue by threatening to go to another firm.

As one lawyer put it, "There's a lot more aggressiveness in the field. The lawyers look at the bankers, who are making reams of money, and at other lawyers who will give what I would call questionable opinions making barrels of money, and they do it, too." There is not as much money in issuing only cautious and conservative opinions.

Nor was Johnson very sanguine about the future when he left the bridge. "I think unless someone is made to suffer" more than the slap on the wrist the IRS has routinely given out when it has been dealing with abuses, "these things are going to continue."

John L. Kraft, a partner at Kraft & McManimon in New Jersey, had some thoughts for the defense in 1990. "Bond counsel have become whipsawed, and whipping boys. At the heart of it you have the Treasury Department, issuing 244 pages of incomprehensible regulations on arbitrage rebate three years after the law has been passed, and only part one of three parts. Yet they raise the specter of taxability from original date of issue."

The arbitrage rebate regulations — once again under reconstruction as of this writing — encouraged legal gunslingers to approach tax considerations "creatively," giving legal opinions based on "relatively far-out interpretations. Investors cannot rely on tax opinions as they can on our opinion of an issue's validity — even reasonable law firms can come to different opinions on the taxability of an issue now, and if they do, how can you say there's no open question?"

The situation does not promise to get any better, and indeed, in 1990, even firms that had rendered only exceptionally conservative opinions were passing on more and more complicated deals designed to skirt arbitrage and various other rules.

The Crazy-Quilt of Regulation

On the federal level, the municipal market is covered by a crazy-quilt of regulators: the Treasury Department, the Securities and Exchange Commission, the Internal Revenue Service, the Supreme Court, and assorted federal courts. A quasi-governmental self-regulatory organization, the Municipal Securities Rulemaking Board, also acts as a regulator. Even the Public Securities Association, a trade group comprised of dealers, occasionally acts the part of a regulator.

The Treasury

The U.S. Treasury kicked off the tax reform craze that did so much to curb the market in the 1980s when in late 1984 it offered a detailed plan to restructure the credit markets.

The Treasury plan, if enacted, would have cut back the then $93 billion tax-exempt market by about two-thirds by strictly prohibiting the sale of tax-exempts designed to help private interests and encouraging corporations to finance their needs through the sale of stock, not bonds.

At the time, Ronald A. Pearlman, assistant Treasury secretary for tax policy, told *Credit Markets* (Dec. 17, 1984), "We want to return the tax exemption for state and local governments to what we believe it was originally intended for, and that was financing true state and local government activities. Period." Pearlman's comments riled many market participants because he and the Treasury saw tax-exemption for municipal bonds not as a constitutional right, but as a form of subsidy that Washington provides state and local governments.

The Treasury tax plan was watered down by Congress. But the department did write the onerous arbitrage-rebate regulations referred to above, and still provides regulatory guidance to the market.

The Internal Revenue Service

The Internal Revenue Service is in charge of collecting the nation's taxes, and its chief interest in the municipal market is making sure that all deals comply with tax law. It has become active in the market as deals have become more complex, fueled both by the Treasury Department's arbitrage rebate rules and higher interest rates.

In modern times, the IRS has routinely threatened issuers of deals it deems abusive with declaring such issues taxable, or blacklisting them. Under a blacklist, the IRS publicly announces that an issuer's nonarbitrage certificates are not to be relied upon, effectively keeping them out of the market because tax-exempt issues are expected to carry such certificates.

In January 1991, the IRS, in a precedent-setting move, notified the Louisiana Public Facilities Authority that it intended to tax bondholders on the interest they received on a $41.6 million multifamily housing bond issue sold by the authority in 1984. The authority said it would fight the action and indemnify any bondholders who were taxed.

Until then, the IRS had not declared any issues taxable, instead reaching cash settlements with issuers. The issuers, in turn, usually settled with the firms that worked on the offending deals.

Many bond lawyers questioned whether the IRS had the power to declare an issue taxable at all. *The Bond Buyer,* in an April 25, 1989, front page story, examined the issue in depth, and noted that from a practical standpoint, most bond lawyers felt that the IRS would never be able to get a court to allow it to tax bondholders, whose only crime was to buy a bond.

But the article added, "Debate over the IRS's enforcement authority is expected to grow as the IRS, along with the Securities and Exchange Commission and the Justice Department, continues to investigate dozens of questionable escrow and black box bond deals that were rushed to market in the mid-1980s to avoid new tax law restrictions. In many of these deals, no projects were built but firms still collected huge fees and arbitrage profits."

The IRS, besides writing tax law, also charges issuers for rulings and opinions that they request — determination letters, opinion letters, and reconsiderations of rulings. The fees range from $50 to $1,000.

The Securities and Exchange Commission

The Securities and Exchange Commission was created by Franklin D. Roosevelt in 1933 as an independent federal regulatory agency whose chief role is to protect investors against fraud in securities sales through civil law enforcement. Perhaps only the Internal Revenue Service, with its threats to declare tax-exempt issues taxable, strikes more fear into the hearts of the municipal market.

Municipal securities are not subject to SEC registration. But in recent years the SEC has taken a more prosecutorial role in its relations with the market. The SEC's wrath was inspired first by the New York City financial crisis in 1975, followed very quickly by the rise of the industrial development bond, the $2.25 billion WPPSS default in 1983 and by Matthews & Wright's "collapsible" bond deals of 1985 and 1986.

What has been noticeable in almost every instance of SEC movement is how long it takes for the agency to come up with an appropriate response, and how little action it actually takes.

In 1983, WPPSS defaulted on $2.25 billion of debt for its nuclear projects 4 and 5. Five years later, in 1988, the SEC issued a 376-page report on the default. It leveled scathing criticisms at all of those involved in the sale and marketing of the bonds, but took no enforcement action.   Instead, the agency published an "interpretive release" which stated that underwriters of all municipal bond issues must have a "reasonable basis for believing in the accuracy of key representations" about the securities they underwrite before bidding on or signing deals. In other words, underwriters would be held accountable for the accuracy of official statements.

The SEC's new disclosure rules, 15c2-12, went into effect on Jan. 1, 1990. They stipulate that before underwriters can bid on or purchase bonds they must obtain and review an official statement from the issuer that is in nearly final form except for such last-minute specifications as ratings. The rule will effect issuers as much as underwriters, and is seen by some observers as the first step toward getting issuers to file detailed annual financial information on their fiscal shape.

The SEC has no legal enforcement power over issuers. But underwriters who violate the rule are subject to administrative action by the SEC, including suspension or revocation of their broker-dealer licenses. So it is in their interest to make sure that the issuers comply.

The first issue to be delayed because of concerns with non-compliance with the SEC rule was a $260 million negotiated issue by the New York State Dormitory Authority, slated for sale on Jan. 10, 1990. The deal was delayed because the official statement did not include updated information on New York State's budget, which at the time was being debated.

The move toward additional disclosure extended to the establishment of "nationally recognized municipal securities information repositories." Dealers that file official statements with a repository would only have to supply copies to customers for 25 days after the end of the underwriting period. Those dealers who do not file them must send hard copies to customers who request them within the first 90 days of issuance.

There are a number of nationally recognized repositories, among them *The Bond Buyer*, J.J. Kenny Co., and Bloomberg Financial. The MSRB is planning to build its own central archive. "The board believes its role is critical because official statements may be needed over a 30- to 40-year period and there is a need to ensure the continuity and usefulness of the collection over this time," the board said in a draft notice to dealers in 1990.

The SEC is dilatory, and at times its behavior is inexplicable. In 1987, the agency issued subpoenas to a score of major underwriters, seeking information on approximately $2.7 billion in what would become known as collapsible escrow bond deals. The deals, the SEC alleged, were sold without reasonable expectation that the projects for which they were issued would ever be built. They were rushed to market to avoid the new arbitrage restrictions placed on much of the market in the 1986 tax act. The understanding was that the proceeds of the deals would be invested or escrowed in higher yielding securities and would later be "collapsed," or called. They were done, in other words, merely to create fees for their underwriters. In most cases, the deals should not have been done at all.

The Bond Buyer conducted an intensive investigation of the 87 deals under SEC scrutiny and found that nearly 90% of them produced nothing tangible. In April 1989, the SEC and Matthews & Wright Group Inc. — the firm at the heart of the investigation — reached settlement over that firm's own 26 sham escrow bond deals. At the time, the agency announced it was continuing its probe of similar abusive deals. But in fact, nothing came of the investigation, which appears to have been dropped entirely. As Washington bureau chief Craig Ferris wrote in the *The Bond Buyer's* "Washington Watch" column, "Keeping that uncertainty hanging over the parties involved may be one way to keep them honest, but it is not fair."

Municipal Securities Rulemaking Board

The MSRB was created by Congress in the Securities Acts Amendments of 1975 to regulate brokers, dealers and dealer banks in municipal securities. The board's rules are subject to SEC approval and administered by the National Association of Securities Dealers. It is funded by fees levied on dealers for each new bond transaction. Currently, the fee is two cents per $1,000 in par value. The board has 15 members, which represent three categories: securities firms, bank dealers and the public.

The MSRB's rules deal comprehensively with five areas of business: professional qualifications; record-keeping; fair practice; confirmation, clearance, and settlement; and disclosure. The MSRB puts together the examination given by the NASD for qualification as registered municipal representatives and principals.

Under terms of a new sunshine rule enacted by the SEC in 1989, details of MSRB arbitration proceedings are released monthly by the organization, sort of a police blotter of the industry.

The MSRB's latest project is the creation of a vast archive of official statements to fulfill the SEC's call for more disclosure in the municipal market.

Congress

The Bond Buyer maintains a large bureau in Washington, D.C., which turns out detailed stories every day on the depredations that the Treasury, the IRS, the SEC and various federal courts wish to visit upon the market. But by far the most mischievous of those in the federal city are those who sit in Congress, and on their tax-writing staffs.

What the municipal market gained from Congress in the 1980s was not incremental change in the treatment of tax-exempts, as had been the norm, but rather a form of regulation by legislation — by persecution, according to some lobbyists. And as long as the nation continues to run $100 billion-plus budget deficits, Congress is likely to remain interested in the market.

The 1980s was the decade of tax reform. In 1983, Sen. Bill Bradley and Rep. Richard Gephardt, both Democrats, proposed a tax reform plan, as did Sen. William Roth and Rep. Jack Kemp, both Republicans. Both of their bills contained new restrictions on tax-exempt finance. In November 1984, the Treasury Department unveiled its own proposal. In 1985, the Reagan administration put forth its own recommendation, also larded with restrictions. In November 1985, the House produced its version of tax reform, known as H.R. 3838, and in 1986, the Senate passed its version. A conference committee worked out differences of opinion, and it was signed into law late in 1986.

As was shown in chapter one, the "reform" — later reformed again in 1989, with some of the curbs eased — effected nearly all areas of tax-exempt finance.

During this period, market participants became well acquainted with the legislative process and found that, more often than not, new ideas on how to regulate the municipal market came not from elected officials but from staff members of Congress's two tax-writing panels: the House Ways and Means Committee, the Senate Finance Committee — each of which have separate Democratic and Republican staffs — and the nonpartisan Joint Tax Committee.

The Supreme Court

The Supreme Court in April 1988 decided the 1982 *South Carolina vs. Baker* case challenging the mandatory registration of the owners of tax-exempt bonds. The court found that registration was constitutional, and then went a step further, throwing out the 1895 *Pollock v. Farmers' Loan & Trust Co.* decision, which gave birth to the doctrine of reciprocal immunity, the legal theory that the federal government cannot tax the debt of state and local governments and vice versa.

The court said, in no uncertain terms, that states have no constitutional right to sell bonds that are tax-exempt. While Congress and the Treasury had been making law pretty much disregarding this precedent, the constitutional safeguard argument was always there, a security blanket for the market.

The Court's decision was 7-1, with Justice Sandra Day O'Connor dissenting. In her dissent, she made a salient point: "If Congress may tax the interest paid on state and local bonds, it may strike at the very heart of state and local governmental activities" and increase their dependence on the federal government. "The Court has failed," she concluded, "to enforce the constitutional safeguards of state autonomy and self-sufficiency that may be found in the Tenth Amendment and the Guarantee Clause, as well as in the principles of federalism implicit in the Constitution." What she marked, plainly, was a fundamental change in constitutional philosophy — that all good, and all benefits, devolve from the State.

At the time, Christopher A. Taylor, executive director of the MSRB, was quoted as saying that municipal issuers "have now been put on the same footing as other recipients of tax breaks. They will have to get in line with the others to argue their case for continuing to receive special treatment.... Congress will be hunting for added revenues next year, and I'm afraid this means that tax-exempt bonds will be like a plump duck flying over the hunting grounds."

Issuers and their various lobbying organizations, in response, stepped up their efforts to ensure that most municipals remain tax-exempt. The PSA estimated, when the court's ruling came out, that if tax-exemption was done away with, it would cost issuers $264 billion extra between now and the year 2000. Several states have passed resolutions for a constitutional amendment protecting tax-exemption.

The Public Securities Association

The Public Securities Association was founded in 1976 but dates from 1912, when the Investment Bankers Association of America was formed. The organization represents more than 400 banks, brokerage firms and associate members in the U.S., United Kingdom and Japan. Its members include all primary dealers in U.S. government securities and 95% of the dealers in municipals. All major dealers in mortgage-backed and money market instruments are also members.

The PSA is a trade group, but at times makes recommendations and prepares legal standards — for repurchase agreements, for example — that carry some weight in the community. It also maintains an extensive lobbying and educational effort in Washington, D.C.

That lobbying effort may have backfired in 1985, when the PSA routinely brought investment bankers to Capitol Hill to lobby against tax-reform proposals, causing congressmen to explode in sputtering fury at the presence of what they saw as at the worst greedy and at the best self-interested professionals — (one recalls Sen. Bob Packwood's 1985 outburst about "these *rich*, a handful of the *richest* law firms," after one such session).

Since then, however, the PSA, along with a number of other municipal lobbying groups, shocked into action after the full impact of the 1986 tax act was appreciated, has specialized in providing the numbers and the testimony of various articulate public officials to congressional committees. The results for the market have been far more salubrious.

A classic example of regulation by the industry itself, and the PSA's role in it, occurred in 1987, when certain escrowed-to-maturity bond issues were threatened with the exercise of call provisions.

The problem stemmed from a $45.81 million issue of special obligation bonds sold on Dec. 4 for the Kansas City, Kansas, Board of Public Utilities. The new bonds restructured certain bonds that were sold in 1982 and escrowed to maturity in 1984. The restructuring specifically allowed the issuer to call the bonds in 1994 instead of from 1997 through 2001, as was stipulated when they were escrowed to maturity.

The issue was negotiated by B.C. Christopher & Co. of Kansas City, Mo., which later acted as financial adviser to the sale of

$93 million special highway obligations. In a rare and concerted effort, the market actually stepped in and "regulated" itself, with dealers vowing not to bid on the highway issue, which was subsequently pulled from the market.

The dealers contended that while the deal might be legal, it would not be ethical, because clients had purchased escrowed-to-maturity bonds "in good faith" — figuring that they were, in fact, escrowed to maturity and noncallable, with their principal and interest payments covered by investments in Treasury securities.

The highway issue would have refunded certain serial bonds sold in January 1985 and escrowed to maturity in November 1985 callable in 1994, their earliest call date, instead of from 1995 through 1999. The bonds, the 8.90s of 1995 and the 9s of 1996 through 1999, had been selling at premium prices, from 115 to 120, but they subsequently fell in price, as did almost all escrowed bonds, generally to a callable price of around 101.

Bond counsel were divided on the issue. Some said that the highway issue would, in fact, be legal, because there was nothing in the original indenture stating that the bonds were not subject to redemption prior to maturity. Others said that the process of escrowing bonds to maturity in essence defeases them, and all of their original call provisions. The counsel on the issue, Gaar & Bell, said the issuers were exercising a call option "that always existed" and that had not been superseded when the bonds were escrowed to maturity. The fact was that nine out of 10 bonds usually have lines in their official statements declaring that the bonds are subject to redemption prior to maturity.

At the time, bankers figured that issuers could save around 300 basis points in interest cost if they called bonds that had been escrowed. At least six states and a number of municipalities were known to be considering deals to call such ETM issues.

The universe of bonds subject to such a call was estimated at anywhere from $10 billion to $50 billion. Dealers were understandably torn between the lure of new business and the fine legal point that they might have been negligent in not specifically telling investors in escrowed bonds that they were also, in fact, callable.

Those on the dealer side, not public finance, carried the day. The highway issue was not brought to market. And in fact only one escrowed issue ever closed, and that in a private placement.

After the Kansas highway issue was pulled, the Texas attorney general's office, responding to a request from the Municipal Advisory Council of Texas (a trade association of dealers in Texas municipal securities) issued a statement saying that bonds sold in Texas that had been escrowed to maturity also were noncallable to maturity, citing 1948 case law as precedent. The letter ruling was made on Dec. 17, 1986. Predictably enough, it was disputed by several lawyers in private.

The MSRB took no immediate action, saying only that dealers had to tell investors *if* bonds were callable, and whether or not the bonds were escrowed to maturity. The *PSA* swung into action almost two months to the day after the problem had surfaced. On Feb. 4, 1987, the group's 44-member executive committee met in New York City and unanimously adopted a resolution urging issuers not to exercise "any possibly perceived rights to call by optional redemption escrowed-to-maturity bonds unless the relevant documentation clearly disclosed that the issuer expressly reserved the right to do so."

This "clearly disclosed" was later privately translated as "not buried back in the legal boilerplate." After all, the redemption provisions of ETM bonds, by virtue of their being printed in the official statement, had in fact been clearly disclosed.

The interpretive statement on this one, on the entire episode, in fact, was that the dealers, seeing that there was the possibility of millions of dollars in lawsuits by angry investors, took it upon themselves to shut down some financings. On the face of it, those financings made economic sense for the issuers. They certainly would have meant substantial fees for the underwriters. But the long-term interests of the market, as judged by the dealers, would not have been served.

A footnote to this episode: The SEC did not issue its own "interpretive letter" on escrowed-to-maturity municipal securities until December 1988. The letter noted only that if issuers wanted to reserve "the contractual right" to exercise optional redemption provisions, then they should disclose it "clearly and conspicuously" both in defeasance notices and in the issuer's official statement for any refunding bonds.

APPENDIX 1:

The History of the Bond Buyer

The Daily Bond Buyer, as it was called until 1982, was founded in 1891 by William Franklin Gore Shanks.

Shanks was born in Shelbyville, Kentucky, in 1837. He was a correspondent for the *New York Herald* during the Civil War and, following the pattern of journalists of the day, he also served as volunteer aide de camp on the staffs of Generals Lovell H. Rousseau and George H. Thomas. He was wounded in the battle of Chickamauga, "from the effects of which he never recovered" in the words of his obituary in 1905.

After the war, Shanks enjoyed a long and illustrious career as a New York City journalist. In 1866, he produced a fat volume of reminiscences of Civil War generals. From 1867 to 1869, he edited *Harper's Weekly.* In 1869, he became city editor of the *New York Times.* In 1870, he joined Horace Greeley's *New York Tribune* and from 1871 to 1880 he was city editor of that paper, where, among other things, he hired the noted reformer Jacob Riis.

As *The Daily Bond Buyer* said in Shanks' obituary, "During that time he made a reputation by his exposure of the corruption in the Supreme Court, which led to the impeachment and removal of Judges Barnard and Cardozo. His life was frequently threatened, and 'Boss' Tweed finally warned him personally to carry a revolver and never to go to his home by the same route two nights in succession.

"During 1871, while fighting the then Democratic rule in Brooklyn, he was locked up in Raymond Street Jail for contempt of court for refusing to disclose the name of a reporter on the *Tribune* who had written an article about a defalcation in a local trust company, the funds stolen having been divided among the 'ring.' He was released on habeus corpus, and the District Attorney, Winchester Britton, who had been the active moving party against him, was removed by Gov. Dix."

Shanks founded the National Press Intelligence Co., a press clipping service, with $50,000 in 1885. He gradually found that there was great demand for "investment news," which led to the founding of *The Daily Bond Buyer* in 1891. In the words of a story about the company published in 1897, "This is simply a daily digest of investment news, being chiefly devoted to early advance news of proposed issues of city, county, state, railway and street railway bonds. . . . Every special election to authorize issues of bonds is reported, the date on which it is to be held being first given, and the result of the vote next carefully noted.

Every advertisement for sealed bids for such bonds is carefully summarized; and, when the bonds are sold, the name and address of the successful bidder is given, together with the amount of the bonds purchased, their rate of interest and term of years they are to run, and all particulars of interest to investors. . . . " With a few alterations, this sums up *The Bond Buyer* of today.

Shanks founded something of a publishing dynasty. He had three sons: Sanders, the attorney of the company; Lynn Hudson Shanks, who was the treasurer; and William Rousseau Shanks. The attorney's son, Sanders Jr., was editor of the newspaper and president of the company from 1914 until his death in 1949, marking the longest stint at the helm so far. The Shanks family was connected with the newspaper until 1977, when William S. Shanks, then president and chief executive officer, severed his connections with the company.

The Daily Bond Buyer went through at least three distinct manifestations during its 100 year history.

First, there was the newspaper of William F.G. Shanks, a small financial daily filled with items culled from various daily newspapers, as well as some of the lively, typically opinionated journalism of the period, no doubt written by the founder himself.

The founder's newspaper covered all of the bond markets: municipal, corporate, Treasury, even foreign securities. In 1904, the newspaper carried a two-page spread, with a map, on "The Japanese in Manchuria," probably as much because Shanks had a long-standing interest in war coverage as because both belligerents floated large loans.

Shanks gave the newspaper a distinctive voice — a decidedly conservative, Republican voice, unabashedly imperialist and frankly partisan. Shanks believed the Democratic Party to be "the greatest curse the nation has known," and used his pages to bang the drum for the Republicans, even going so far as to produce a pamphlet in 1904 containing "some wholesome truths not generally taught in schools and colleges of the present day"—that Thomas Jefferson was, in fact, the first Republican president of the U.S., and that Madison, Monroe and Adams were also early members of the GOP.

Shanks was also fond of protecting his new paper from the competition, and regularly included in *The Daily Bond Buyer* what he sometimes termed "The Deadly Acrostic," an item of bond news arranged so that, in November 1897, for example, the first letter in each item, if read down the column, spelled FILCHED.

For years he warred in this way against the competition, in particular the *American Banker,* from whom he won $5,500 in libel verdicts, $5,000 in 1898 when the owners of the *Banker* said he was blackmailing municipal bond dealers, and $500 in 1897 when the same parties alleged that he was "a man of bad habits."

The *American Banker,* in its battles with Shanks, won six cents, along with six cents for costs in a 1900 libel suit after a jury asked whether or not it could bring in a verdict for the defendant.

The municipal bond market of the founding Shanks' era was litigious, and the newspaper devoted a lot of space to lawsuits, especially in regard to repudiated debt and invalidly issued debt. It also carried a fair number of articles on counterfeiting and security, and even did a supplement to its weekly publication (then called simply *The Bond Buyer)* about safes and how easy they were to open—with the lone exception of the Corliss safe, a globe-shaped contraption which the newspaper heartily endorsed.

These were the years when municipal bond volume was measured in the hundreds of millions of dollars, not billions. When the newspaper was founded, volume barely totaled $50 million, and the newspaper did not officially begin tallying it until 1896, when 1,294 municipal bond issues totaling $119.54 million were sold. In 1905, when the founding Shanks died, long-term volume was $197.70 million. It would not break the $1 billion mark until 1921—and dipped below that line in 1932, 1937, and from 1942 to 1945.

The Daily Bond Buyer took on the issues of the day, and those issues in Shanks' time included "repudiation" of debt and the rise of "postage-stamp" and "pool" bidders.

Postage-stamp bidders were so-called because they bragged they could bid on a bond deal with no capital and no office—just a postage stamp or post card sent to the issuer. If the postage-stamp bidder won the bonds and then sold them, nobody was the wiser. But if the market turned on him, the bidder could, and apparently did with some frequency, walk away from deals.

There were also, in the woollier days of the municipal bond market, "poolers." As *The Daily Bond Buyer* defined them: "'Poolers' are men who usually have no capital and little standing, who seek every opportunity to be 'bought off' by other bidders by threatening to run up the bidding at sales to figures which leave no margin for profit."

The newspaper said that the way to combat such rascals in the market was not to demand a good faith check in advance of a bond sale, but rather to demand such a check *after* the bonds were awarded. As the newspaper editorialized in 1897, "We hoped and believe that the City Treasurer of Boston had furnished a solution when, not having exacted a deposit preliminary to bidding, he required a large deposit before officially announcing an award to a house whose ability he had reason to doubt."

The newspaper continued, "We shall believe that the adoption of such a rule by all Municipalities"—that is, only requiring checks if the highest bidder is unknown to the issuer—"would encourage bidding while at the same time protecting sellers of bonds from imposition. The present system requires a deposit from every house bidding, though only one check can by any possibility be retained: and as a consequence, many times the deposit named has to be drawn from a bank and remain idle, not drawing interest, pending this sale. It often happens that each dealer is simultaneously called upon for several guarantee deposits, so that in the aggregate the idle money represented by these checks is a very considerable sum, and the annual loss in interest an onerous and needless tax."

As the editor wrote, nearly a century ago: "It really is in the interest of Municipalities that the submission of guarantee checks should be done away with; as the bids for bonds are likely, in the absence of such requirements, to be more numerous. [This, by the way, was in an era when 117 bids on one issue was not entirely unknown.] The Municipal authorities have merely to stipulate that they reserve the right to reject any bid, and to demand a deposit if the highest bidder is unknown to them or known to be irresponsible."

Yet it must be said that Shanks was definitely a man of his time, complete with its prejudices. He cheered a Luzerne County, Pa., sheriff, for example, for firing into the ranks of some Hungarian-born rioters, and noted with smug satisfaction, "Such ignorant races as Hungarians, Italians,

Greeks, and Spaniards ought to be excluded from the country by an amendment to our immigration laws. Skin a Hun, Italian, Greek, Spaniard or Cuban and you disclose a Barbarian."

Shanks died in Bermuda in 1905 and with him, with a few exceptions, went the first age of the newspaper. His successor was his son William R., who served until 1914, when the paper was taken over by his son, Sanders Shanks, who ran it until 1949. The Shanks family sold a controlling interest in the newspaper to C. Barron Otis in 1913. Otis then bought the *American Banker* in 1918.

During this period, the paper had relatively few sparks of journalistic glory; it devoted itself to gathering statistics and covering federal assaults on tax-exemption.

The lone exception was the "Travis Inquiry," begun by the newspaper and taken up independently by the *Brooklyn Daily Times.* As editor Sanders Shanks wrote in 1920, "Prior to June, 1916, many rumors reached us via the New York financial district of the existence of a 'system' which monopolized the State's investment business to the exclusion of a majority of the legitimate bond houses and incidentally profited unduly on the large amounts of securities purchased annually by the State with tax monies appropriated to sinking funds for the protection of holders of State obligations. . . ."

The Daily Bond Buyer, having gotten its "lead" in the classic journalistic way — from sources — proceeded to do some hard nuts and bolts work and proved that the comptroller, one Eugene M. Travis, authorized purchases of bonds from only two dealers: Albert Judson and Geo. B. Gibbons & Co., and that the purchases were done at inflated prices that turned Judson a profit of $825,141.65.

In 1920, Travis, his assistant, James A. Wendall and Judson were charged with grand larceny, but the indictment was dismissed in October 1921 by the state Supreme Court. Wendall won election as comptroller in 1920 and died in 1922. The newspaper professed its own bitter disappointment, and noted, "If public officials, entrusted with the custody and management of millions of dollars of public funds raised by taxation and held in trust for the owners of the State's bonds, may conduct themselves as did Travis and Wendall with respect to the investment of some $40 million within a period of less than six years, we cannot help but view with the gravest apprehension the future security of the State Sinking Funds and the many large issues of State bonds which depend upon the standing of these funds for their prompt payment at maturity."

The newspaper continued, "To the lay mind it would appear inconceivable that the Court should ask for any more complete array of evidence indicative of criminal intent upon the part of the three defendants than the ample proof showing that time and again huge blocks of bonds were purchased at prices which the three defendants by their own admission must have known were substantially in excess of actual market values."

The episode marked the newspaper's last foray into investigative journalism for 60 years.

The Daily Bond Buyer was not always marked by journalistic excellence. The only things that transcended what would be an almost uninterrupted snooze from the founder's death to the 1960s were its numerous defenses of tax-exemption, described in Chapter I, and the quality of its statistics.

The newspaper, as noted above in "The Deadly Acrostic" episode, was jealous of the information it gathered in its columns of proposed bond issues, sealed bids and bond sale results. It gathered this data into monthly tables—and for a few decades, put bond sales and volume figures into "pink sheet" supplements.

The newspaper began its famed indexes, which measure yields on municipal bonds, in 1917, and retroactively figured them to 1900. The 20-general obligation bond index was calculated annually through 1914, although its first appearance in the newspaper was apparently not until in 1918. The higher-grade 11-bond index started in 1915. Both indexes were calculated four times a year in 1915 and 1916.

In 1917, the newspaper began calculating its 20- and 11-GO bond indexes on the first day of each month. It would do so until 1946, when it changed the frequency to weekly.

The 20-bond index, measuring yields of GO bonds maturing in 20 years, has a rating roughly equivalent to Moody's A1; 11 of the same bonds are used to calculate the 11-bond GO index, which is rated roughly equivalent to Moody's Aa.

For those with a taste for trivia, the record high of the 20-bond was 13.44%, which it hit on Jan. 14, 1982; the record low was 1.29%, which it posted on Feb. 14, 1946. The record high of the 11-bond index was 13.05%, which it hit on Jan. 14, 1982; the record low was 1.04%. The greatest movement in the indexes took place in 1980. On Feb. 22 of that year, the 20-bond index jumped 71 basis points, to 8.46%. On April 18, it plunged 118 basis points, to 7.89%; the 11-bond barometer fell 129 basis points, to 7.32%.

The newspaper introduced its revenue bond index — which uses 25 assorted revenue bonds maturing in 30 years, ranging from Baa1 to Aaa in rating — on Sept. 20, 1979. Its record high was 14.32%, on Jan. 14, 1982; its low was 6.92%, on March 5, 1987.

To accompany its bond yield indexes, the newspaper began a short-term tax-exempt note index in 1989, using yields from 10 issuers.

Beginning in December 1927, the newspaper began compiling every Friday "The Visible Supply of Municipals," which presented "the total volume of offerings of state and municipal issues, excluding short-term notes, as listed in our "Calendar of Sealed Bid Offerings."

Yet *The Daily Bond Buyer* for almost four decades, from the 1920s to the 1950s, was little more than a municipal bond man's "shopper." The front page was devoted to dealer advertisements—and would be until the 1950s. During the 1920s and 1930s, entire weeks would go by without any actual stories. The stock market crash in October 1929 was not even mentioned in the daily until Nov. 27 —and then only in a brief report on a Guaranty Trust Co. survey.

What little editorial copy there was during the 1920s was generally picked up from other sources. A 1921 story, "The Bond Business as an Occupation for College Men," was reprinted from *The Outlook* magazine; coverage of a Florida hurricane in October 1926 was provided by a visiting bond dealer.

Even at this editorially low point, however, the newspaper managed to stay in touch with its market, even if the articles were sparse. For example, *The Daily Bond Buyer* in March 1928 produced its first roundup of top municipal bond underwriters. The year was a good one for bond volume—$1.48 billion in 7,748 issues, the seventh consecutive year tax-exempt volume topped $1 billion. The author of the story noted, "We have analyzed the activities of the dealers participating in these underwritings and find that 82 houses were identified with the original offerings of issues aggregating $20 million or more; 65 houses were named in connection with issues of $50 million or more; and 19 appeared in underwritings aggregating more than

$100 million. The largest total shown for any one house is $254.43 million."

The tabulation of the top underwriters was done on the basis of full credit to each manager—"the total for any one house is merely the aggregate of the entire amounts of all the issues with which that dealer was associated." Eldredge & Co. topped the 1927 underwriters, with $254 million to its credit, and it was followed by Detroit Co., with $215.29 million. First National Bank of New York was third, at $199.28 million, followed by Redmond & Co., at $197.99 million; National City Co., $175.53 million; Stone & Webster and Blodget, $171.35 million; Phelps, Fenn & Co., $161.66 million; Bankers Trust, $151.57 million; Old Colony Corp., $150.42 million; and Kissel, Kinnicutt & Co., $142.43 million.

It was an interesting idea, ranking underwriters. But, for reasons lost now, the newspaper would not carry another list of underwriter rankings for more than 50 years.

The newspaper also noted the rise of "the Street broker," what we today call the brokers' broker, in 1928; decried "service contracts"—sort of a precursor to negotiated transactions—in 1926; and the "street improvement assessment bond evil"— what later became known as tax increment financing—in 1927.

To follow the economic situation in the 1930s, the newspaper carried a regular column of notices on "Debt readjustments, refunding plans, and defaults" beginning in 1934. During the Depression, 4,770 municipal governments defaulted on $2.85 billion in debt, about 16% of debt outstanding in 1932.

Still, there was relatively little editorial comment or analysis of the situation. Editor Sanders Shanks reprinted a speech of his own on municipal bond defaults and how they were being remedied. In September 1934, the newspaper noted, "One of the outstanding features of the municipal bond business these days is the activity of those bankers, bond attorneys and others who are participating in the working out of debt adjustments . . . Due to economic recovery, plus successful negotiation between debtor and creditor, many municipalities of importance have moved or soon will move out of the default classification. A brief review of this situation may be timely. . . ."

More typical of the day's coverage, such as it was, was the report of a "special correspondent" who provided coverage of a 1933 counterfeiting scheme in Kansas which forced Gov. Alf Landon to suspend all interest payments on the state's municipal bonds. Providing a flavor of the period, one guest author asked in 1933, "What Will Repeal [of Prohibition] Do For Municipal Finance?" The author's conclusion was that it would restore local taxes. "With repeal, the increase in internal revenue taxes and license fees will make the old 15-cent drink a thing of the past. Instead, the prices will probably be 25 to 35 cents; but even these will look cheap compared to the speakeasy prices."

The 1940s brought with them perhaps the most concentrated attacks on tax-exemption. To keep its readers informed on the battle, *The Daily Bond Buyer* carried a weekly "Washington Letter" on Saturdays. In addition, the paper began carrying a municipal market column, also on Saturdays. There was little news printed during the week—with the result that there was no mention of the attack on Pearl Harbor in 1941 until Dec. 13, and then only in the municipal market column. "The concussion from the Japanese bombs which fell on Pearl Harbor last Sunday," it said, "caused the greatest disturbance experienced by the municipal market since the beginning of World War II in September, 1939. . . . it is difficult to measure precisely the decline in prices."

Besides a listing devoted to "Municipal Men in Military Service" and an occasional letter from one of them at the front, the war had little impact on *The Daily Bond Buyer*.

But it did have an impact on interest rates, as shown in a timeline the newspaper put together in November 1945. The timeline, "Municipal Market During World War II," represented a first for the newspaper. It showed 20-bond index yields, in response to various events, falling from 3.21% at the opening of the war in 1939 to 1.64% at the end.

During the 1940s, the municipal market managed to fight back assaults on tax-exempt bonds by no less than the president of the United States and the chairman of the Federal Reserve Board.

President Franklin Roosevelt told Congress in 1942 that it "seems right and just that no further tax-exempt bonds should be issued." He added that, "as a matter of equity, I recommend legislation to tax all future issues of this character."

Roosevelt, in fact, sent his Treasury Secretary, Robert Morgenthau, to Capitol Hill several times with proposals to tax the interest of newly issued municipals. He had the support of Federal Reserve Board chairman Mariner S. Eccles, who tried unsuccessfully to persuade associations representing local government officials to back FDR's legislation, arguing that they didn't need the subsidy inherent in tax-exempt bonds.

But an editorial in *The Daily Bond Buyer* took issue with that argument, describing how cities were under financial stress "during the dark days of World War II" and accusing Eccles of "wearing his rose-tinted glasses" when he made his statement.

Although Congress rejected several bond taxation proposals during the 1940s, *The Bond Buyer* predicted that "the matter is going to come up again and again until it is finally settled by a Supreme Court ruling."

Some in the municipal market thought they got just such a ruling in 1945. Four years before, the Treasury Department taxed holders of bonds issued by the New York Port Authority, saying that the authority was not a political subdivision and therefore not eligible to issue tax-exempt debt. The U.S. Tax Court in 1944 reversed the IRS action, and the Supreme Court declined to hear the case in 1945.

"Judging by the reaction of the municipal bond market to the denial of a review of the Port case, municipal bond buyers feel that the threat of taxation is now pretty completely removed," said an editorial in *The Daily Bond Buyer* after the high court's ruling. But the newspaper itself was much less sanguine, saying that "there is no indication" that the ruling "ends the matter."

The 1950s saw *The Daily Bond Buyer* cease Saturday publication and undergo a redesign of its nameplate, along the way to entering its third, modern age, in which it presented its readers with a wild gallimaufry of material. There was no more Washington Letter, but the paper began coverage of the U.S. Treasury market, picking up a column from the *American Banker* called "Speaking of Government Securities." It also carried, for the first time, an editor's column, "Now—And Then," by George Wanders, later to be changed to "From the Editor's Desk," which is what the same column is called today.

The newspaper, which began the decade with advertisements on its front page and ended it with editorial material once again capturing Page 1, carried a number of singularly odd features, all of which died quick deaths: "Women in Municipal Bonds," featuring photographs of women who worked for bond firms; "Odd Lots of Municipal News," and "Well-Known Bond Men and Municipal Officials Visiting in New York."

The newspaper entered its modern era, its third age, if you will, only in the 1960s, with regular coverage of the municipal and Treasury bond markets and news stories dominating page one. In a sense, *The Bond Buyer* of today more closely resembles *The Daily Bond Buyer* of the founder's day than it does the newspaper of the 1920s through the 1950s. The newspaper returned to being a truly journalistic enterprise, rather than just a trade paper.

News stories began to dominate page one, although the advertisements would not disappear entirely until the late 1970s. The paper began adding bureaus during this time, always an indication of a newspaper with serious journalistic intentions. It opened one in Washington in 1960 and then, in rapid succession, San Francisco in 1982, Chicago and Atlanta in 1987, and Dallas in 1990. And a regular editorial page was established.

Much of the "modern" history of this period in the paper's life is covered in this book: the collapse of New York City, the Tax Reform Act of 1986, the WPPSS default, the explosion of rates and volume that characterized the 1980s. The newspaper began its second hundred years in 1991, inarguably at its height in terms of journalistic quality.

APPENDIX 2:

The Tax Reform Act of 1986

Following are the main provisions of the Tax Reform Act of 1986, as it applied to tax-exempt municipal bonds.

I. Private Activity Bonds

Interest on all private activity municipal bonds will be taxable unless they fall under the exempt category of "qualified bonds." A bond is considered to be for a private activity when more than 10% of the issue's proceeds are used for any private business, and when the payment of principal or interest on more than 10% of the issue is secured by property used by a private business.

II. Qualified private activity bonds that retained their tax-exemption include:

1) Exempt facility bonds
a) Airports
b) Docks and wharves
c) Mass commuting facilities
d) Sewage disposal facilities
e) Solid waste disposal facilities
f) Facilities for furnishing electric energy or gas
g) Facilities for furnishing water
h) District heating or cooling facilities
i) Qualified hazardous waste facilities
2) Multifamily housing bonds
3) Single-family housing bonds
4) Qualified 501(c)(3) bonds
a) Hospitals are qualified but the term "hospital" does not include rest or nursing homes, day care centers, medical school facilities, research laboratories or ambulatory care facilities. Also, the weighed averaged maturity of qualified 501(c)(3) bonds may not exceed 120% of the economic life of the property.
5) Qualified redevelopment bonds
This covers tax increment financing in which in the course of redevelopment a project is generally transferred to private individuals.
6) Qualified student loan bonds

III. Unified Volume Limitation for Private Activity Bonds:
To further limit the issuance of private activity bonds, the Tax
Reform Act imposed the following cap:

a) A single unified volume limitation will be applied to all
private activity bonds including multifamily and single-
family housing bonds. Qualified veterans mortgage bonds will
retain their own separate volume limitation. Those areas
which do not come under the limitation are: general
obligations, qualified 501(c)(3) bonds, airports, docks and
wharves, government-owned solid waste disposal facilities and
current refunding issues.

b) The annual ceiling per state in 1986 and 1987 will be $75
per capita or $250 million, which ever is greater. After 1987 the
annual ceiling will be $50 per capita or $150 million,
whichever is greater.

c) 50% of the volume limitations will be allocated to state
agencies, and the remaining 50% shall be allocated to local
issuers in proportion to population.

d) 95% of the "net proceeds" of all issues of private activity
bonds must be used for the exempt purpose of the borrowings.
The 5% balance of the issue must include the cost of issuance.
Also, the issuance cost may not exceed 2% of the face amount of
the issue. This amount is increased to 3.5% for qualified
mortgage bonds when the face amount does not exceed $20
million. This limits the amount of "spread" or profit that
investment bankers can work into a deal.

IV. Advanced Refunding Reductions

a) For bonds issued before January 1, 1986, the refunding
bonds must be the first or second advance refunding of the
original bond unless the bonds were advance refunded two or
more times before March 14, 1986, in which case a transition
rule will permit one additional advance refunding.

b) For bonds originally issued after December 31, 1985, the
refunding bond must be the first refunding of the original bond.

c) For bonds originally issued before January 1, 1986, the
refunded bonds are required to be redeemed not later than the
earliest date on which such bond could be redeemed at par or a
premium of 3% or less if the advanced refunding will produce a
debt service savings.

d) For bonds originally issued after December 31, 1985, the refunded bond is required to be redeemed not later than the first date on which its call is not prohibited in the case of a refunding producing debt service savings.

V. Current Refundings

Current refunding bonds may not exceed the outstanding amount of the refunded bonds, and the maturity date of such refunding bonds may not exceed the later of the maturity date of the refunded bond or the date that is 32 years after the date of issuance of the refunded bonds.

VI. Alternative Minimum Tax (AMT)

Private activity bonds issued after August 7, 1986, are treated as preference items for those eligible for the A.M.T. Exceptions to the rule are qualified 501(c)(3) bonds and current refunding bonds if the refunded bond was issued before Aug. 8, 1986.

Also, if a corporation's book income (which includes all tax-exempt income) exceeds its taxable income, 50% of the difference becomes a tax preference for the AMT.

Example:

$1,100,000 (Book income)

$1,000,000 (Taxable income)

$100,000 (Difference)

50% or $50,000 becomes a tax preference item for AMT. That $50,000 can include tax-exempt income (GOs and revenue bonds of any issue date).

VII. Property and Casualty Insurance Companies

The deduction taken for losses incurred by property and casualty insurance companies is reduced. This is equal to 15% of tax-exempt interest received or accrued during the taxable year. This applies to all municipal bonds acquired after Aug. 7, 1986, and is effective with respect to taxable years beginning after Dec. 31, 1985.

VIII. Bank Deduction

The act eliminated commercial banks' ability to deduct 80% of the interest they incur to carry their tax-exempt investment portfolios. Exceptions were made to protect smaller municipalities throughout the nation which depended on local banks to purchase their bond issues. Banks are permitted the deduction on "Bank qualified municipal bonds," which are bonds issued by a municipality whose total issuance for the calendar year will not exceed $10 million.

APPENDIX 3:

The Rating Agencies

Following are the symbols used by the three rating agencies active in the municipal bond market: Moody's Investors Service, Standard & Poor's Corp. and Fitch Investors Service. The agencies charge issuers a fee for their ratings, and generally insist that the issuers keep them updated on their fiscal condition.

MOODY'S INVESTORS SERVICE

1. Bond ratings

Aaa—Best-quality bonds. They carry the smallest degree of investment risk and are generally referred to as "gilt-edged." Interest payments are protected by a large or an exceptionally stable margin and principal is secure. While the various protective elements are likely to change, such changes as can be visualized are most unlikely to impair the fundamentally strong position of such issues.

Aa—Bonds of high quality by all standards. Together with the Aaa group they comprise what are generally known as high-grade bonds. They are rated lower than the best bonds because margins of protection may not be as large as in Aaa securities or fluctuation of protective elements may be of greater amplitude, or there may be other elements present which make the long-term risks appear somewhat larger than in Aaa securities. The strongest bonds in this class are rated **Aa1.**

A—These bonds possess many favorable investment attributes and are to be considered as upper medium-grade obligations. Factors giving security to principal and interest are considered adequate, but elements may be present that suggest a susceptibility to impairment in the future. The strongest bonds in this class are rated **A1.**

Baa—Medium-grade obligations; they are neither highly protected nor poorly secured. Interest payments and principal security appear adequate for the present but certain protective elements may be lacking or may be characteristically unreliable over a great length of time. Such bonds lack outstanding investment characteristics and in fact have speculative characteristics as well. The strongest bonds in this class are rated **Baa1.** This is the lowest category considered investment grade.

Ba—These bonds are judged to have speculative elements; their future cannot be considered as well assured. Often the protection of interest and principal payments may be very moderate and therefore not well safeguarded during both good and bad times in the future. Uncertainty of position characterizes bonds in this class. The strongest bonds in this class are rated **Ba1.**

B—These bonds generally lack characteristics of the desirable investment. Assurance of interest and principal payments or of maintenance of other terms of the contract over any long period of time may be small. The strongest bonds in this class are rated **B1.**

Caa—These bonds are of poor standing. Such issues may be in default or there may be present elements of danger with respect to principal or interest.

Ca—These bonds are speculative to a high degree. Such issues are often in default or have other marked shortcomings.

C—The lowest rated class of bonds. Issues so rated can be regarded as having extremely poor prospects of ever attaining any real investment standing.

Con.(-)--- Conditional. Bonds for which the security depends upon the completion of some act or the fulfillment of some condition carry this prefix. These are bonds secured by (a) earnings of projects under construction, (b) earnings of projects unseasoned in operating experience, (c) rentals that begin when facilities are completed or (d) payments to which some other limiting condition attaches. The parenthetical rating denotes probable credit stature upon completion of construction or elimination of basis of condition.

2. Short-term securities and loan ratings

MIG-1/VMIG-1—This designation denotes best quality. There is present strong protection by established cash flows, superior liquidity support or demonstrated broad-based access to the market for refinancing.

MIG-2/VMIG-2—This designation denotes high quality. Margins of protection are ample although not so large as in the preceding group.

MIG-3-VMIG-3—This designation denotes favorable quality. All security elements are accounted for but there is lacking the undeniable strength of the preceding grades. Liquidity and cash flow protection may be narrow and market access for refinancing is likely to be less well established.

MIG-4-VMIG-4—This designation denotes adequate quality. Protection commonly regarded as required of an investment security is present and although not distinctly or predominantly speculative, there is specific risk.

S.G.—This designation denotes speculative quality. Debt instruments in this category lack margins of protection.

3. Commercial paper ratings

The term "commercial paper" means promissory obligations having original maturity of up to nine months. The ratings are opinions of the ability of issuers to repay punctually.

Prime-1— Issuers (or related supporting institutions) rated Prime-1 have a superior capacity for repayment of short-term promissory obligations. Repayment capacity will normally be evidenced by the following characteristics: 1) Leading market positions in well-established industries; 2) High rates of return on funds employed; 3) Conservative capitalization structures with moderate reliance on debt and ample asset protection; 4) Broad margins in earnings coverage of fixed financial charges and high internal cash generation; 5) Well-established access to a range of financial markets and assured sources of alternate liquidity.

Prime-2 —Have a strong capacity for repayment. This will normally be evidenced by many of the characteristics cited above but to a lesser degree. Earnings trends and coverage ratios, while sound, will be more subject to variation. Capitalization characteristics, while still appropriate, may be more affected by external conditions. Ample alternate liquidity is maintained.

Prime-3 —Have an acceptable capacity for repayment. The effect of industry characteristics and market composition may be more pronounced. Variability in earnings and profitability may result in changes in the level of debt protection measurements and the requirement for relatively high financial leverage. Adequate alternate liquidity is maintained.

Not Prime— Issuers in this category do not fall within any of the Prime rating categories.

STANDARD & POOR'S CORP.

1. Bond ratings

AAA—The highest rating assigned to a debt obligation. Capacity to pay interest and repay principal is extremely strong.

AA—Bonds rated AA have very strong capacity to pay interest and repay principal and differ from the highest rated issues only to a small degree. The strongest bonds in this category are rated **AA-plus,** the weakest, **AA-minus**.

A—Bonds rated A have a strong capacity to pay interest and repay principal, although they are somewhat more susceptible to the adverse effects of changes in circumstances and economic conditions than bonds in higher rated categories. The strongest bonds in this category are rated **A-plus,** the weakest, **A-minus.**

BBB—Bonds rated BBB are regarded as having an adequate capacity to pay interest and repay principal. Whereas they normally exhibit adequate protection parameters, adverse economic conditions or changing circumstances are more likely to lead to a weakened capacity to pay interest and repay principal for bonds in this category than for bonds in higher rated categories. The strongest bonds in this category are rated **BBB-plus,** the weakest, **BBB-minus.**

BB, B, CCC, CC—Bonds rated BB, B, CCC and CC are regarded, on balance, as predominantly speculative with respect to capacity to pay interest and repay principal in accordance with the terms of the obligation. BB indicates the lowest degree of speculation and CC the highest degree of speculation. While such bonds will likely have some quality and protective characteristics, these are outweighed by large uncertainties or major risk exposures to adverse conditions. Plus and minus are also used in these categories to indicate relative standing.

C—Reserved for income bonds on which no interest is being paid.

D—Bonds are in default, and payment of interest and/or repayment of principal is in arrears.

2. Note ratings

SP-1—A very strong or strong capacity to pay principal and interest. Issues determined to possess overwhelming safety characteristics will be given an **SP-1-plus** rating.

SP-2—A satisfactory capacity to pay principal and interest.

SP-3—A speculative capacity to pay principal and interest.

3. Commercial paper ratings

A—Issue has the greatest capacity for timely payment. Issues in this category are delineated with the numbers 1, 2 and 3 to indicate the relative degree of safety:

A1— Degree of safety regarding timely payment is either overwhelming or very strong. Those issues determined to possess overwhelming safety characteristics will be denoted **A1-plus.**

A2— Capacity for timely payment is strong. However, the relative degree of safety is not as strong as for issues designated A1.

A3—The issue has a satisfactory capacity for timely payment. However, it is somewhat more vulnerable to the adverse effects of changes in circumstances than obligations carrying the higher ratings.

B—The issue has only an adequate capacity for timely payment. Such capacity may be damaged by changing conditions or short-term adversities.

C—A short-term obligation with a doubtful capacity for payment.

D—Issue is either in default or is expected to be in default upon maturity.

FITCH INVESTORS SERVICE INC.

1. Bond ratings

AAA—Bonds are considered to be investment grade and of the highest quality. The obligor has an extraordinary ability to pay interest and repay principal which is unlikely to be affected by reasonably foreseeable events.

AA—Bonds are considered to be investment grade and of high quality. The obligor's ability to pay interest and repay principal, while very strong, is somewhat less than for AAA securities or more subject to possible change over the term of the issue.

A—Bonds are considered to be investment grade and of good quality. The obligor's ability to pay interest and repay principal is considered to be strong, but may be more vulnerable to adverse changes in economic conditions and circumstances than bonds with higher ratings.

BBB—Bonds are considered to be investment grade and of satisfactory quality. The obligor's ability to pay interest and repay principal is considered to be adequate. Adverse changes in economic conditions and circumstances, however, are more likely to weaken this ability than bonds with higher ratings.

BB—Bonds are considered speculative and of low investment grade. The obligor's ability to repay principal is not strong and is considered likely to be affected over time by adverse economic changes.

B—Bonds are considered highly speculative. Bonds in this class are lightly protected as to the obligor's ability to pay interest over the life of the issue and repay principal when due.

CCC—Bonds may have certain characteristics which, with the passing of time, could lead to the possibility of default on either principal or interest payments.

CC—Bonds are minimally protected. Default in payment of interest and/or principal seems probable.

C—Bonds are in actual or imminent default in payment of interest or principal.

DDD, DD, D—Bonds are in default and in arrears in interest and/or principal payments. Such bonds are extremely speculative and should be valued only on the basis of their value in liquidation or reorganization of the obligor.

Plus and **minus** are used after a rating to designate the relative position of a credit within the rating grade. They are carried in ratings from AA to B.

NR indicates that either Fitch has not been requested to rate the specific issue or that a review of the rating has not taken place within Fitch's current schedule for updating ratings.

Suspended—A rating is suspended when Fitch deems the amount of information available from the issuer to be inadequate for rating purposes. A rating may also be suspended when situations arise such as certain types of litigations, governmental actions or environmental concerns, the outcome of which is uncertain but has the potential to cause a serious adverse impact on an issuer's current or future financial condition.

Withdrawn—A rating is withdrawn at Fitch's discretion when an issuer fails to furnish proper and timely information, when an issue matures, is called or refinanced, or when it does not appear in the best interests of the investor for Fitch to maintain a rating.

Conditional—A conditional rating assumes the timely and successful completion of the project being financed by the debt securities being rated and indicates that the payment of debt service requirements is largely or entirely dependent upon the successful completion of the project. In addition, in the case of a start-up facility, the rating may also indicate that the payment of the debt service requirements is dependent upon the achievement of a level of operations consistent with that forecast in the feasibility study.

2. Commercial Paper Ratings

Fitch-1—Commercial paper assigned this rating is regarded as having the strongest degree of assurance for timely payment.

Fitch-2—Issues assigned this rating reflect an assurance of timely payment only slightly less in degree than the strongest issues.

Fitch-3—Commercial paper carrying this rating has a satisfactory degree of assurance for timely payment but the margin of safety is not as great as the two higher categories.

Fitch-4—Issues carrying this rating have characteristics suggesting that the degree of assurance for timely payment is minimal and is susceptible to near-term adverse change due to less favorable financial or economic conditions.

LOC—This symbol following any of the above grades indicates that a letter of credit issued by a commercial bank is attached to the commercial paper note. The noteholder is the direct beneficiary of the bank's obligation to use its own funds to pay the full amount of the note at maturity at the time such action is required by the terms of the letter of credit. Other commercial paper programs supported by a bank letter of credit but where the letter of credit is not attached to the commercial paper note do no carry this designation.

GLOSSARY OF MUNICIPAL BOND TERMS

A

Acceleration—A provision, normally present in a bond indenture agreement, mortgage or other contact, that the unpaid balance is to become due and payable if specified events of default should occur. Such events include failure to meet interest, principal or sinking fund payments; insolvency; and nonpayment of taxes on mortgaged property.

Account—The members of an underwriting syndicate.

Accretion of a Discount—An accounting procedure that reflects the increase in a security's value at maturity, when it is purchased at a discount.

Accrued Interest—The amount of interest accumulated, on a daily basis, since the last payment date and up to the delivery date, paid to a new holder by the seller of a bond.

Accumulation Account—A portfolio of securities purchased by the sponsor of a unit investment trust, just before the trust is formally established.

Acquired Obligations—A term used in IRS regulations to describe obligations allocated to an issue's proceeds during the time it is outstanding.

Acquired Purpose Obligations—A term used in IRS regulations to describe loans taken out to carry out a municipality's governmental programs.

Active Market— Heavy volume of trading in a particular stock, bond or commodity. The spread between bid and asked prices is usually narrower in an active market than when trading is quiet.

Ad Valorem Tax—A tax based on the value of property.

Additional Bonds Test—A legal requirement that new additional bonds, that will have a claim to revenues already pledged to outstanding revenue bonds, can only be issued if certain financial or other requirements are met.

Advance Refunding—A method of providing for payment of debt service on a municipal bond until the first call date or maturity from funds other than an issuer's revenues. Advance refundings are done by issuing a new municipal bond and investing the proceeds in a portfolio of U.S. government securities structured to provide enough cash flow to pay debt service on the refunded bonds. The old issue can then be said to be advance refunded.

Do not confuse advance refunding with **defeasance,** which eliminates the issuer's legal obligation to a bond issue. Bonds can be advance refunded but still be the issuer's obligation until they are redeemed.

After-Tax Yield—The annual yield figured as a yield to maturity, adjusted for capital gains taxes.

Agency Cross—A purchase and sale handled by one dealer acting as agent for both seller and buyer.

Agreement Among Underwriters—The contract set up between members of an underwriting syndicate, stipulating the activities of each member.

All or None—An offering requiring the buyer to buy or bid for all of the securities offered.

Amortization—The elimination of debt through scheduled payments.

Amortization of Premium—An accounting process showing how the book value of a security purchased at a premium declines during its life, so that at maturity its purchase price is par.

Annual Return—Total return on a security, expressed as an annual percentage rate.

Any Interest Date Call—A call feature under which the issuer may redeem outstanding securities on any interest payment date, after the first call date.

Appropriation—An authorization by a legislative body to set aside cash for a specific purpose.

Arbitrage—The practice of simultaneously buying and selling an item in different markets to profit from a spread in prices or yields resulting from market conditions. Examples of arbitrage include buying foreign currency at a certain rate on one exchange and selling it at a different rate on another exchange.

In municipal bonds, arbitrage profits are made by selling tax-exempt bonds and investing the proceeds in higher-yielding taxable securities. Municipal issuers are allowed to make arbitrage profits under certain, restricted conditions, but Section 103(c) of the Internal Revenue Code prohibits the sale of tax-exempt bonds primarily for the purpose of making arbitrage profits; these illegal bonds are called *arbitrage bonds.*

Arbitration—Under MSRB rules, two parties who have a disagreement involving a municipal securities transaction may submit the disagreement to an impartial panel for resolution.

Artifice or Device—A term used in section 103 of the IRS code to describe a transaction that enables the issuer to gain arbitrage profits.

As Agent Trade—A securities transaction done by a dealer on behalf of another party.

Asked—The price sellers put on their bonds.

Assessed Valuation—The valuation placed on property for purposes of taxation.

Associated Person—A professional at a broker or dealer.

Atlanta Lawsuit. Filed on Aug. 31, 1987, by Georgia, the city of Atlanta, the Government Finance Officers Association and the National League of Cities in the U.S. District Court for the Northern District of Georgia. It challenges the constitutionality of the Tax Reform Act of 1986's arbitrage rebate requirement and alternative minimum tax provisions. The tax law's arbitrage rebate rule requires all municipal bond issuers to rebate any arbitrage profits they earn on tax-exempt bond proceeds to the Treasury, unless they qualify for either of two narrow exemptions. Previous law placed a rebate requirement only on arbitrage profits of industrial development bonds.

The law also subjects interest earned from most newly issued industrial development bonds to both individual and corporate minimum taxes. In addition, half of a corporation's book profits, including interest earned on tax-exempt bonds, are subject to the minimum tax at an effective rate of 10%. Interest earned by individuals from general obligation bonds is still exempt from the minimum tax.

Auction Bid—A bidding procedure run as an auction, where bonds are awarded to the highest bidder. Bonds awarded this way are said to be competitively bid, or just competitive issues.

Authentication—When a bank or trust company certifies that the signature and seal of an issuer are valid.

Authority—A unit or agency of a municipality established to perform a single function or group of activities, usually supported by user fees.

Authorization Ordinance—A law that allows a governmental unit to sell a specific bond issue or finance a specific project.

Average Effective Interest Cost—The average interest rate on a bond issue, including issuance costs, expressed as either Net Interest Cost or True Interest Cost (*which see)*.

Average Life (bonds). The average length of time an issue of serial bonds and/or term bonds with mandatory sinking funds and/or estimated prepayments are expected to be outstanding.

B

Baby Bond—1. A denomination issued in less than $1,000; also known as a mini-bond. 2. A bond issued by the state of Louisiana during Reconstruction, featuring the portrait of a baby on its face.

Balance—The number of bonds remaining in a new deal.

Balloon Maturity—An inordinately large amount of bond principal which matures in a single year.

Balloon payment—A large loan principal payment on a single date.

Bank Underwriting—Current law allows banks to underwrite general obligation bonds and certain revenue bonds, such as bonds for public education and housing facilities. See **Glass-Steagall Act.**

Basis Book—A book of mathematical tables used to convert yields to dollar prices.

Basis Point— One-100th of a percentage point. It is used most often to describe changes in yields on bonds, notes and other fixed-income securities. For example, a rise in yield from 8% to 8.15% is an increase of 15 basis points.

Basis Price—The price of a security expressed in yield.

Bearer Bond—A bond that is payable to the holder; such a bond does not carry the owner's name. The federal government proscribed issuance of tax-exempt bearer bonds after June 1, 1983. Prior to that date, most municipal bonds were issued in bearer form; however the Internal Revenue Code requires most tax-exempt securities issued after that date to be **registered**. Private placements and issues maturing in one year or less are exempted.

Beneficial Owner—The person to whom benefits of an investment accrue, even though it is held in the name of another person or a firm.

Best Effort—An offering not sold as as a whole, but just as what can be sold.

Bid—1. The price offered by prospective purchasers of securities. When a nonexchange-traded security's price is quoted, the bid is usually used; sometimes the price is given as two numbers: the first is the bid, the second is the asked (the price at which a security is offered for sale).

2. An offer from an underwriter to a municipal issuer in a competitive bond offering, or an offer to purchase Treasury securities. See **competitive bid.**

Bid Form—A document on which underwriters state their proposed interest rates and price for a deal.

Bid Wanted—A listing of securities put out by a dealer, asking for bids on some or all of them.

Bidding Limitations—Restrictions placed by the issuer on the kinds of bids it will accept: range of rates, discounts, etc.

Black-Box Deal—A deal in which a mortgage broker is supposed to find a separate source of money to fund a guaranteed investment contract to secure the bonds. That separate source comes from the sale of the developer's promissory note. It allows the bond proceeds to be turned over to the developer to construct the project. In black box deals there are two streams of money: the bond proceeds are supposed to be used to build projects and another source of cash — to be obtained from the sale of shares in the mortgage note on the project property —is supposed to be used to purchase credit enhancement. But in abusive deals, there are no investors for the mortgage note and the bond proceeds are used to purchase GICs, thereby assuring there is no money for the projects.

Blind Pool—In a blind pool, neither the specific participants nor the exact amounts they wish to borrow have been determined. The bonds are generally issued by a single locality based on a survey of other localities that might want to participate at some point in the future. Blind pools differ from so-called dedicated pools, in which all participants and the specific amount they want to borrow are spelled out before the issue goes to market.

The bonds tend to be long-term (30 years or more) and are designed to earn arbitrage. Under pre-1986 tax law, blind pool issues could earn arbitrage for up to three years. During that time, municipalities could repay the money earned and keep the profits. As a result, other municipalities could reborrow the money and earn more arbitrage, because the three-year limit wasn't reached.

Block—A large number of bonds offered for sale.

Blow-Out—A new issue which sells out immediately.

Blue List—A daily Standard & Poor's Corp. publication of municipal bonds offered for sale in the secondary market by various dealers. The Blue List volume is the total par value of all bonds offered for sale in *The Blue List of Current Municipal Offerings.*

Blue Sky law—A general term referring to various state laws enacted to protect the public against securities fraud. These laws describe the method and form of registration of municipal bonds in each particular state.

Boilerplate—Commonly repeated legal sections of an official statement or other agreement, which do not vary between similar transactions.

Bond—Interest-bearing certificate issued by governments and corporations when they borrow money. The issuer agrees to pay a fixed principal sum on a specified date (the maturity date) and at a specified rate of interest.

In measuring municipal bond volume, a bond is a security maturing more than one year from issuance; shorter-term obligations are usually termed notes or commercial paper. In the Treasury market, bonds mature in more than 10 years, notes in less than 10 years but more than one year, and bills in one year or less. Municipal bonds are denominated in units of $1,000 par value.

Bond and interest record—The record maintained for each bond issue showing the amounts of interest and principal due on each payment date, and related information.

Bond Anticipation Note (Ban)—A kind of short-term debt that is retired with proceeds from a subsequent bond sale.

Bond Banks—State bond banks buy issues from localities and sell larger offerings. This arrangement cuts borrowing costs for the local issuers because the bond banks' debt usually carries higher ratings than that of the municipalities, whose issues are usually too small to be rated anyway. Credit enhancements, such as bond insurance, are also cheaper when purchased for larger issues. Localities' use of the bond banks is voluntary.

Bond banks have operated in Canadian provinces since the 1940s. Vermont established the first state bond bank in 1969.

Bond Buyer Index—Generally used to connote *The Bond Buyer's* index of yields on 20 general obligation bonds, calculated weekly. The index, of GO bonds maturing in 20 years, has a rating roughly equivalent of A1. Eleven of the same bonds are used to calculate the 11-bond GO index, which has the rough equivalent of a double-A.

The 20- and 11-bond indexes were compiled on the first day of each month from 1917 to 1946; since then they have been compiled weekly. The record high for the 20-bond was 13.44%, which it hit on Jan. 14, 1982. The record low was 1.29%, which it posted on Feb. 14, 1946. The record high for the 11-bond index was 13.05%, which it hit on Jan. 14, 1982; the record low was 1.04%.

The Bond Buyer also has a revenue bond index, which uses 25 assorted revenue bonds, maturing in 30 years, ranging from Baa1 to Aaa in rating. The index was started on Sept. 20, 1979. Its record high was 14.32%, on Jan. 14, 1982; its low was 6.92% on March 5, 1987.

A short-term tax-exempt note index was begun in 1989. It is calculated using 10 note issuers: California, Colorado, Idaho, New York State, Pennsylvania, Texas, Wisconsin, Los Angeles County, New York City and Philadelphia.

Bond Buyer Municipal Bond Index—An index of bond prices designed by the Chicago Board of Trade for trading long-term municipal bond futures. The index is compiled Monday through Friday by *The Bond Buyer.*

The index uses price quotes on 40 recently marketed municipal bonds, known as The Bond Buyer 40. The bonds are priced and evaluated at about 3 p.m. by six municipal dealer-to-dealer brokers (Cantor, Fitzgerald Municipal Brokers Inc., Chapdelaine & Co., Clifford Drake & Co., J.F. Hartfield & Co.,

O'Brien & Shepard Inc. and Titus & Donnelly Inc.). The four middle quotes are then divided by a conversion factor derived from the amount at which the bond would be priced to yield 8%. The converted prices, or index prices, are added and averaged. The average is multiplied by a "composition" coefficient, designed to compensate for changes in the list of 40 bonds, to obtain the index's reading for the day, which is quoted in points and 32ds, such as 79-05.

The bonds on the list are selected and changed twice a month. The securities are the 40 most recent term issues that meet the following criteria: The principal amount must be at least $50 million, except for housing bonds for which a $75 million minimum applies. Each issue must be rated at least A by Moody's Investors Service or A-minus by Standard & Poor's Corp. Each bond must mature in no less than 19 years, have a first call in no less than seven and no more than 16 years, and be callable at par. A bond's initial reoffering price must be between 95 and 105. No more than two bonds from an issuer may be included. Because of the special call features common to housing issues, a housing bond will be dropped form the index if it is quoted at 102 or higher on the two consecutive days preceding a list revision. Variable-rate bonds, put bonds, and other bonds with special features are not eligible.

On each day that the list is changed, the index values of the old and new lists are calculated and the old list's value divided by the new list's to produce the composition coefficient for the next two weeks.

The current dollar prices of the Bond Buyer 40 are also added and averaged to obtain an average dollar price. The yield of the Bond Buyer 40 is computed from the average price, the average coupon and the average maturity represented by the date of each issue's first call at par.

Bond Contract—Terms of the agreement between issuer and buyer, typically including the bond resolution, trust indenture and various security provisions.

Bond Counsel—A lawyer who reviews the legal documents and writes an opinion on the security, tax-exempt status and issuance authority of a bond or note.

Bond Election—The process by which voters approve or reject bond issues.

Bond Equivalent Yield — Also known as coupon equivalent yield. The return on a discounted security, such as a zero coupon bond, figured on a basis which permits comparison with regular interest-bearing securities.

Bond Fiscal Year—The 12-month period used in connection with certain bonds, not necessarily the issuer's fiscal year.

Bond Fund—A portfolio of municipal bonds that offers shares to investors either through closed-end funds or unit investment trusts (*which see*), which offer shares of fixed portfolios of municipal bonds; or through open-ended, managed, or mutual funds, which offer shares in managed portfolios of municipal bonds whose size will vary as shares are purchased or redeemed.

Net asset value of a share in a fund is determined by calculating the market value of the fund's portfolio assets, deducting all management expenses, and then dividing by the number of shares outstanding.

Bond Insurance—Insurance purchased by an issuer for either an entire issue or specific maturities, which guarantees the payment of principal and/or interest. This security usually provides a higher credit rating and thus a lower borrowing cost for an issuer.

Bond Point—1% of the face value of a bond or note. Since bonds are denominated in $1,000, one bond point equals $10.

Bond Premium. The amount at which a bond or note is bought or sold above its par value without including accrued interest.

Bond Power—A document attached to a registered securities certificate used in lieu of an assignment form to authorize the transfer of securities.

Bond Prices—Prices are given in fractions per 100 rather than dollars and cents. A price of $973.75 for a $1,000 bond is given as 97 3/8.

Bond Proceeds—The money the issuer receives from its bond sale.

Bond Purchase Agreement—The contract between the issuer and the underwriter setting the terms, prices and conditions of the sale.

Bond Ratings—The series of letters, numbers, and symbols used by the bond rating agencies to designate the credit quality of a bond issuer's securities.

Bond Register—A record, kept by a transfer agent or registrar on behalf of an issuer, of the names and addresses of registered bond owners.

Bond Resolution—A legal document describing in specific detail the terms and conditions of a bond offering, the rights of the bondholder and the obligations of the issuer to the bondholder. The document is alternatively referred to as an **indenture of trust.**

Bond Transcript—The legal documents associated with a bond offering.

Bond Year—$1,000 of debt outstanding for one year. The number of bond years in an issue is the number of bonds times the number of years from the dated date to maturity. The number of bond years is used in calculating the average life of an issue and its net interest cost.

Bonded Debt—The portion of of an issuer's total indebtedness as represented by outstanding bonds.

Direct or Gross Bonded Debt—The sum of the total bonded debt and short-term debt.

Net Direct Debt or Bonded Debt—Direct debt less sinking fund accumulations and all self-supporting debt.

Total Overall Debt or Total Direct and Overlapping Debt—Total direct debt plus the issuer's applicable share of the total debt of all overlapping jurisdictions.

Net Overall Debt or Net Direct and Overlapping Debt—Net direct debt plus the issuer's applicable share of the total debt of all overlapping jurisdictions.

Overlapping Debt—The issuer's share of the debt of other local units.

Book—Presale orders for a new bond issue, based on preliminary price levels. For example, a bond dealer says his company has a *book* for $60 million of the $75 million term bonds of 2014. In a negotiated offering, one syndicate manager (usually but not always the lead manager) keeps track of the members' positions in the sale and is said to be *running the books.*

Book-Entry and Book-Entry Securities—Securities in the form of entries (usually computerized) in the issuer's or a clearing house's books, as opposed to being printed in physical certificates with coupons that must be clipped for cashing. Almost all U.S. government and agency securities are sold in book-entry form, but not many municipal bond issues have been book-entry issues. Mandatory registration of municipal bonds is expected to lead to more book-entry sales because the privacy of unregistered **bearer** bonds is lost.

Book Value—The value at which a security is shown on the holder's balance sheet. Can include amortization or accretion and will frequently differ from market value.

Broker's Broker—A broker that deals only with other municipal securities brokers and dealers, not with retail investors.

C

Calendar—A list of upcoming offerings.

Call—For issuers, to redeem a bond prior to maturity.

Callable Bond—A bond or note subject to redemption at the issuer's option prior to its stated maturity.

Call Price—The price at which a bond will be redeemed if called, usually around 101 or 102.

Canadian Interest Cost (CIC)—A method of calculating the interest cost, as a percentage, of a bond issue. It is not used as frequently as the **net interest cost** method .

Capital Accumulator Bond—A variation of the zero coupon bond that is purchased at face value and pays principal and all accrued interest at maturity. The yield to maturity is fixed, as with a zero coupon bond.

Capital Appreciation Bond— Same as **capital accumulator bond** and **compound interest bond.**

Capital Gain—The profit realized when a security is sold at a higher price than which it was purchased.

Carry—The interest cost of financing a portfolio or an inventory of securities.

Chapter 9. The section of federal bankruptcy law under which municipalities may file for protection from creditors.

Close-Out—A procedure which permits dealers which have purchased securities but not yet received them to take action to complete the transaction.

Closing—The procedure by which a sale between the issuer and the buying group is completed. It is at the closing that the issuer delivers the securities to buyers and the issuer receives the proceeds from the sale of securities.

Cogeneration—The use of industrial waste heat for electrical power.

Collateralized Annuity Bonds (CABs) — These bonds amortize in the same way a mortgage does, with scheduled level payments comprising principal and interest. The bonds cannot be called.

Commercial Paper—Unsecured promissory obligations issued by corporations and municipal governments, typically for a short period (up to 270 days). Corporate paper is taxable while municipal paper is tax-exempt.

The U.S. Supreme Court ruled in July 1984 that commercial paper is a security rather than the "functional equivalent" of a loan.

Committee on Uniform Securities Identification Procedures assigns the CUSIP numbers to securities. The numbers identify each maturity of an issue. The committee was set up by the American Bankers Association and is now run by Standard & Poor's Corp.

Comfort Letter—A letter from an independent accountant providing the latest financial information on an issuer, delivered when a new issue is sold.

Competitive Bid—A sealed bid tendered in a Treasury or municipal auction by an underwriter or investor for a specific amount of securities at a specific yield or price. Noncompetitive bidders, which appear mostly in Treasury auctions, agree to pay the average of all bid prices.

Compound Interest Bond — See **capital accumulator bond** and **capital appreciation bond.**

Concession—Discount off the reoffering or list price of a bond or note that is given to dealers and dealer banks.

Conduit Financing—The sale of bonds or notes by a governmental unit for the benefit of a third party, usually a private corporation. The securities issues are not considered general obligations of the conduit agency.

Confirmation—Written statement provided to customers detailing transactions.

Coupon, Coupon Rate—**Coupons** are attached to bond certificates; they are removed (clipped) and presented to paying agents for payment, usually semiannually. The **coupon rate** is the rate of interest stated on a bond to be paid by the issuer to the purchaser; it is based on the face value of the security. A **coupon bond** often used interchangably with **bearer bond** as opposed to a **registered bond.** But a coupon bond may have registered principal and unregistered coupons.

Prior to July 1983, most municipal bonds were issued in coupon form; however, the Internal Revenue Code requires most tax-exempt securities issued after that date to be registered. Private placements and issues maturing in one year or less are exempted.

Covenant—A legally binding commitment by the issuer of municipal bonds to the bondholder.

Cover—The differential in basis points between the first and the second bid in a competitive underwriting. The second-best bid.

Coverage—The the margin of safety for payment of debt service on a revenue bond that reflects the number of times the actual or estimated project earnings or income for a 12-month period exceed debt service that is payable.

Credit Watch—A designation by Standard & Poor's. The agency places securities on CreditWatch with either negative or positive implications for from three to six months as a temporary classification while a credit is under review.

Current Coupon—Securities selling close to par value.

Current Yield—The ratio of the annual interest paid to the price of a security. For example, a $1,000 bond purchased at par, with a 6.50% coupon, would have a current yield of 6.50%.

CUSIP—Committee on Uniform Securities Identification Procedures *(which see)*. The committee was formed to create a method of identifying securities. Each maturity of an issue has a CUSIP number.

D

Dated Date—The date carried on the face of a municipal bond or note from which interest normally begins to accrue. The dated date is usually, but not always, the issue date; it is printed on the bonds in anticipation that the bond issue will be sold without delay so that the dated date and issue date coincide. If for some reason a bond issue is dated but not sold until after its first coupon comes due, the coupon can be voided and clipped. For bonds sold after the dated date but before the first coupon date, the underwriters usually pay the issuer the appropriate accrued interest and charge the final buyers (who will receive the full coupon payment).

Dealer—A corporation or partnership that buys, sells and maintains an ongoing position in bonds or notes, or both.

Dealer Bank—A commercial bank that maintains an underwriting and trading presence in tax-exempt debt.

Debentures—In the corporate securities market, debentures are interest-bearing certificates that, unlike bonds, are not backed by physical assets of the corporation. If a bond issue goes into default, the holder has some claim to the property of the issuer. If a debenture goes into default, the holder has no claim. An unsecured bond is a debenture. A debenture is documented by an agreement called an indenture.

Debt Limit—The legal maximum debt-incurring power of a municipality. Can also be called the debt ceiling.

Debt Offsets—Money and other assets in sinking and reserve funds held to redeem long-term debt.

Debt Per Capita—Bonds divided by population.

Debt Ratio—The ratio of an issuer's debt outstanding to a measure of property value.

Debt Service—Required payments for principal and interest.

Debt Service Reserve Fund—A fund created by a bond indenture and held by the trustee, usually amounting to principal and interest payment for one year, and used only if normal revenues are not sufficient to pay debt service.

Deep Discount Bonds—Bonds selling for far less than their face value, generally less than 80% of par. **Discount** bonds sell for less than face value. A deep discount bond will have a yield or return well above the stated coupon rate. The difference between the discount price and the redemption price is subject to federal capital gains tax.

Default — The failure to make timely payment of interest or principal on a debt instrument; or the occurrence of an event as stipulated in the indenture of trust resulting in an abrogation of that agreement. An issuer does not default until it fails to make a payment.

Defeasance—Bonds for which the payment of principal and interest has been assured through the structuring of a portfolio of government securities, the principal and interest on which will be sufficient to pay debt service on the refunded, outstanding bonds. When a bond issue is defeased, the claim on the revenues of the issuer is eliminated and the debt can be wiped off the issuer's books.

Delivery—The time when payment is made to, and the executed bonds and notes are received from, the issuer. New-issue delivery takes place several weeks after the sale to allow the bonds and notes to be printed and signed.

Demand Notes—Securities that can be sold by the holder back to the issuer (or its designated agent) on short notice, usually seven days. Demand notes can have maturities as long as 30 years, but the "resale on demand" feature allows them to carry yields of short-term notes. Most demand notes also carry variable rates.

De minimis Provision— A provision of the 1987 tax bill that would have modified a 1972 Internal Revenue Service ruling that said the agency would not trace whether a corporation has violated the IRS' prohibition on incurring debt to buy tax-exempt securities if the firm's holdings of tax-exempt debt total no more than 2% of its assets. The House tax bill would have changed the cutoff level to the lesser of 2% or $1 million.

Denomination—The face or par amount that the issuer promises to pay at a specific bond or note maturity.

Depository— A clearing agency which provides immobilization, safe-keeping and book-entry settlement services to its customers.

Designated Order— A large order given by a reputable institutional investor in which the buyer denotes preference to certain dealers in the underwriting group and gives them credit for the sale of a specific amount of bonds out of the total.

Direct Debt—The debt a municipality incurs in its own name.

Direct Placement—The same as **private placement,** in which a new issue is sold directly to one or several institutional investors instead of being offered publicly through underwriters.

Discount—The amount in dollars by which the market value of a bond is less than its par value.

Discount Bonds—Bonds selling for less than their face value; compare **deep discount** bonds. A discounted bond will have a yield or return above the stated coupon rate. The difference between the discount price and the redemption price is subject to federal capital gains tax.

There are also **original-issue discount** securities, which are issued at an offering price substantially below par. Unlike discount bonds, the appreciation from the original price to par over the life of the OID bond is treated as tax-exempt income.

Discount Note—A noninterest-bearing note sold at a discount and maturing at par. The U.S. Treasury sells three-month, six-month and one-year bills in this fashion.

Discount Rate—The interest rate paid by financial institutions when they borrow from the Federal Reserve Bank.

Displacement—Municipal bonds scheduled for sale but which have not been sold.

Divided Account—A form of underwriting account in which a member's liability ceases when he has taken down an amount of bonds equal to his participation. Also known as a "Western" account.

Dollar Bonds—Bonds that are quoted in terms of price rather than yield. Dollar bonds are long-term maturities of substantial size (usually $50 million and up). They are predominantly revenue bonds, although some are general obligations.

The price of a dollar bond is expressed in dollars and eighths of a dollar per $100 of face value. A price of 94 3/8, for example, equals $94.375 per $100 face value, or $943.75 for each $1,000 bond. Bonds selling at prices below 100 are said to be selling at a discount; bonds selling at prices over 100 are selling at a premium.

Double-barreled bond—A bond with two distinct pledged sources of revenue, such as earmarked monies from a specific enterprise or aid payments as well as the general obligation taxing power of the issuer.

Double-Exempt—A security free from taxation from two different entities, such as state and federal government.

Downgrade—A reduction in a credit rating.

Due Diligence—The investigation of a bond issue, by underwriter's and issuer's counsel, to ensure that all material facts relating to the issue have been disclosed to potential buyers in the official statement.

Duration—The sum of the present values of each of the principal and interest payments of a security, weighted by the time to receipt of each payment, divided by the total of the present values of the payments. Unlike average life or average maturity, duration takes into account the timing of both principal and interest payments.

Dutch Auction—An auction, usually done in conjunction with short-term securities, at which investors stipulate the lowest rate they will accept.

E

Eastern Account—This is the most popular bond syndicate account and it is universal in the eastern part of the U.S. In this account, a participant's liability in a bond issue is undivided. Even though a member may take down and sell bonds greater in number than its participation, it still has its proportional liability for the number of unsold bonds left in the account.

Effective Interest Cost—The rate at which the debt service on bonds would be discounted to provide a present value equal to the bid amount on the bonds.

Effective Interest Rate—The actual rate of interest earned by an investor, based on the price paid for the bond, coupon, maturity and time between interest dates.

Enterprise Debt—Debt which will be retired by the revenues earned by a facility.

Equal Annual Maturity Bonds—Serial bond issues in which the amount of principal paid is about the same each year.

Equivalent Bond Yield—The annualized yield on a short-term discount security expressed on a comparable basis to yields on interest bearing securities.

Equivalent Taxable Yield—What a taxable security would have to yield to provide an investor with the same after-tax return he could earn on a tax-exempt security.

Escrow Account—A fund that can be used only to pay debt service.

F

Face Amount—The par value of a bond.

Facsimile Signature—The reproduction of a signature by engraving, stamping or other means.

Fail Position—Securities undelivered due to the failure of selling clients to deliver the securities to their brokers so the latter can deliver them to the buying brokers. Since brokers are constantly buying and selling, receiving and delivering, the term usually refers to a net delivery position—a given broker owes more securities to other brokers on sell transactions than other brokers owe to it on buy transactions.

Fail to Deliver— A situation where the broker-dealer on the sell side of a contract has not delivered securities to the broker-dealer on the buy side. A fail to deliver is usually the result of a broker not receiving delivery from its selling customer. As long as a fail to deliver exists, the seller will not receive payment.

Fail to Receive—A situation where the broker-dealer on the buy side of a contract has not received delivery of securities from the broker-dealer on the sell side. As long as a fail to receive exists, the buyer will not make payment for the securities.

Farmers Home Administration—A Department of Agriculture agency that makes loans to farm owners or tenants, or guarantees loans to such borrowers.

Feasibility Study—A report by an independent expert on the economic need and practicality of a proposed program

Federal Funds (rate). Loans between member banks of the Federal Reserve System. They are used to stabilize surpluses and deficiencies in required reserves among the banks and in transactions requiring immediately available funds. The money is borrowed overnight at a rate known as the federal funds rate.

Fiduciary—An entrusted individual or institution.

Financial Adviser—Advises an issuer on financial matters pertaining to a proposed securities issue. Not usually part of the underwriting group.

Firm Price—A price a dealer says will not be changed for a specified period of time.

Fiscal Agent—A bank chosen by a borrower to perform certain functions related to the sale and administration of a securities issue.

Fiscal Biennium—Some state and local governments organize their budgets for two-year fiscal periods known as fiscal bienniums. These periods rarely correspond to the calendar year.

Fiscal Year. The federal government and most state and local governments use fiscal years that do not correspond to the calendar (January to December) year.

Fixed Interest Rate Put Option Bonds—Bonds that pay a fixed interest rate until the first put option date, when the fixed rate is set again.

Flat—1) In bond trading, without accrued interest. This means that accrued interest will be received by the buyer if and when paid but that no accrued interest is payable to the seller. Issues in default and income bonds are normally quoted and traded flat. The opposite of a flat bond is an *and interest* bond. 2) Inventory of a market maker with a net zero position, i.e., neither long nor short. 3) Position of an underwriter whose account is completely sold.

Flip—The sale of securities shortly after their purchase.

Float—The dollar amount of securities in the **Blue List.**

Floater—A security sold with a floating or variable interest rate, which changes at intervals ranging from daily to annually.

Floating Rate Put Option Bond—A bond bearing a variable interest rate which also allows holders to put it back to the issuer. Such bonds are backed by letters of credit or similar liquidity facilities.

Flow of Funds—The process stipulated in bond documents for collection and disbursal of pledged revenues.

Focus Report—A report summarizing a firm's financial and operational condition. The acronym stands for Financial and Operational Combined Uniform Single report.

Full Disclosure—The complete details of a transaction, contained in a municipal new issue's official statement, that potential investors would consider before deciding whether or not to buy a security.

Full Faith and Credit—The pledge of the general taxing power of a government to pay its debt obligations.

G

General Obligation Bond— A security backed by the full faith and credit of a municipality.

Glass-Steagall Act of 1933—The federal Banking Act of 1933. Major provisions created the Federal Reserve System's Open Market Committee and the Federal Deposit Insurance Corp., and separated commercial banking from investment banking.

Global Certificate—A single certificate representing an entire issue of securities, kept at a depository or book-entry agent.

Going Away—Bonds purchased by investors rather than dealers for inventory.

Good Delivery—A delivery of securities where all legal details are in order.

Good Faith Deposit—A sum of money, usually 2% of the par value of an issue of securities, given by bidders to issuers when they bid for competitive deals. The sum, usually given as a cashier's or certified check, is returned to the bidder if the bid is rejected.

Governmental Accounting Standards Board—Established by the Financial Accounting Foundation, the board writes accounting procedures for governmental bodies that, after approval by the federal government, become generally accepted accounting principles.

Government Finance Officers Association—A professional organization of state and local government finance officers, formerly known as the Municipal Finance Officers Association.

Government National Mortgage Association. Founded in 1968, the association is part of the U.S. Department of Housing and Urban Development. It issues pass-through securities, nicknamed Ginnie Maes, backed by pools of Federal Housing Administration and Veterans Administration mortgages. Unlike the Federal National Mortgage Association and the Federal Home Loan Mortgage Corp., Ginnie Mae securities are backed by the full faith and credit of the U.S.

Grant Anticipation Notes— Short-term debt that is secured by grant money expected to be received after the debt is issued.

Gross Revenues—Revenues of an issuer prior to the payment of expenses for operation, maintenance and debt service.

Group—An underwriting account formed for the purpose of bidding or negotiating the purchase of a new bond offering.

Group Net Order—An order confirmed to the buyer where the sales credits benefit all members of the underwriting group.

Guaranteed Investment Contract—In a guaranteed investment contract, a financial institution, usually a life insurance company, provides the issuer with a guaranteed rate of return that is slightly higher than the interest rate on the bonds, thus allowing the issuer to earn arbitrage profits. The repayment of the bonds is dependent primarily on the ability of the insurance company to honor that contract, and not on any loans made by the issuer.

H

Haircut—A term in the securities industry referring to the formulas used in the valuation of securities for the purpose of calculating broker-dealers' net capital. The haircut varies according to the class of a security, its market risk and the time to maturity.

High-Grade Bonds—Top-rated bonds, usually triple-A rated.

Hospital Revenue Bonds—Bonds issued by a municipal or state agency to finance construction of a hospital or nursing home. The latter is then operated under lease by a not-for-profit organization or a for-profit corporation. A hospital revenue bond, which is a variation on the **industrial development bond,** is tax-exempt, but there may be limits to the exemption.

Housing Bonds—Bond issued by a municipal or state agency to finance construction of housing, and secured by mortgage revenues. There are two types of housing revenue bonds, single-family, sold to provide residential mortgages, and multi-family, sold to construct apartment buildings.

Housing Project Notes—Short-term securities sold by the Department of Housing and Urban Development for public housing agencies around the country. The auctions of HUD notes have been suspended since August 1984.

Humphrey-Hawkins Act (of 1978)—The federal law officially titled the Full Employment and Balanced Growth Act of 1978. Among other things, it (1) requires the President to include in his annual economic report numerical short goals for the current year and next three years for unemployment, production, real income, productivity and prices, and (2) requires the Federal Reserve Board to report twice a year on its monetary policies and their relationships to the growth and employment goals of the act, with the second report each year to include predictions for economic conditions in the next calendar year.

I

Indenture—A legal document describing in specific detail the terms and conditions of a bond offering, the rights of the bondholder, and the obligations of the issuer to the bondholder. The document is alternatively referred to as a bond resolution or deed of trust. It covers such considerations as: 1) form of the bonds; 2) amount of the issue; 3) property pledged (if not a debenture); 4) protective covenants including any provision for a sinking fund; 5) working capital and current ratio; and 6) redemption rights or call privileges. The indenture also provides for the appointment of a trustee to act on behalf of the bondholders, in accordance with the Trust Indenture Act of 1939.

Industrial Development Bond—Also called **industrial revenue bond;** the two terms are generally interchangeable in ordinary contexts, but follow the issuer's preference in references to specific securities. IDBs are tax-exempt bonds issued by a public agency to finance qualifying facilities for private enterprises, such as water and air pollution control, ports, airports, resource-recovery plants and housing. The bonds are usually repaid by revenues from the corporate beneficiary. Most IDBs are issued by authorities established by state or local governments; the agencies (and not the governmental bodies that set them up) are actually responsible for debt service.

The first modern IDB was created in 1936 in Mississippi, under terms of the state's Balance Agriculture with Industry Act; the town of Durant sold the first issue, $85,000 to help bring a hosiery plant to the city.

Initial Offering Price—The price based upon yield to maturity and expressed as a percentage of par at which the underwriter offers the bonds.

Institutional—Signifying banks, financial institutions, bond funds, insurance companies and others who operate in the bond market, as opposed to **retail**, or individual buyers.

Interchangeable (Bond)-- A bond that can be either registered or in bearer form at the option of the purchaser and may be changed from one form to the other. Such bonds now exist only in the secondary market; new issues have been banned since July 1, 1983.

Interest—The amount paid by borrowers on the funds they borrow.

Interest Claim—A request that a person who received an interest payment but who was not entitled to it forward it to the rightful recipient, which could arise if a registered security was sold and the new owner had not yet been recorded when an interest payment was made.

Interest Rate Swap—An agreement between two parties to exchange future flows of interest payments. One party agrees to pay the other at a fixed rate; the other pays the first party at an adjustable rate that is usually tied to the London interbank offered rate, a benchmark rate representing the amount paid by major European banks on dollar-denominated deposits.

Interim Borrowing—Short-term loans taken in anticipation of tax collection or bond sales.

Intermediate Range—Securities with maturities of between six and 15 years.

Inverted Yield Curve—When short-term interest rates are higher than long-term rates.

Investment Grade—Designation given by a national rating service if it includes a bond in one of its top four categories, from AAA/Aaa to BBB/Baa. Many states require fiduciaries (trustees, administrators, executors, etc.) to invest only in securities with investment-grade ratings.

Investment Letter—In the private placement of new securities, a letter of intent between the issuer of securities and the buyer establishing that the securities are being bought as an investment and are not for resale. This is necessary to avoid having to register the securities with the Securities and Exchange Commission. (Under provisions of SEC Rule 144, a purchaser of such securities may eventually resell them to the public if certain specific conditions are met, including a minimum holding period of at least two years.) Use of the investment letter gave rise to the terms letter stock and letter bond in referring to unregistered issues. See also **letter security.**

Issuance Costs—The costs incurred by the issuer in connection with its offering. These include underwriter spread, feasibility studies and various professional fees.

J

Joint Account—An underwriting account formed by two or more dealers.

Joint-Action Agency—A group of municipal utilities that have joined together to provide services more economically than they could do individually. Most joint-action agencies are for generating and distributing electricity, although there are also some joint-action agencies for water and sewerage. Usually, the agencies are formed to build a specific plant or plants; these are generally funded by municipal obligations backed by take-or-pay or take-and-pay contracts with the participating utilities.

Joint and Several Obligation—A form of contract in which each of the signers is obligated for the full contract amount if other signers should default.

Junior Lien Bonds—Bonds with a subordinate claim against pledged revenues.

Junk Bonds—Bonds rated below investment grade, lower than Baa by Moody's and BBB by Standard & Poor's.

L

Lease—A conditional sales agreement under which a municipal government leases equipment, using borrowed funds, that it acquires at the end of the lease period. The loans are backed by the equipment itself and are renegotiated annually.

Lease Rental Bonds—Bonds, the principal and interest on which are payable exclusively from rental payments from a lessee. Rental payments are often derived from earnings of an enterprise that may be operated by the lessee or the lessor. Rental payments may also be derived from taxes levied by the lessee.

Legal Investments—Investments which municipal governments, or private companies acting as fiduciaries, can make under law.

Legal Opinion—The written conclusion of of a lawyer trained in municipal bond law that the bond complies with bond law, especially with regard to its tax-exempt status.

Letter of Credit— A form of supplemental (or, in some cases, direct) security for municipal bonds, under which commercial banks or private corporations guarantee payments on the bond issue under specified conditions.

Letters of Confirmation—Letter confirming the formation and obligation of the members of an underwriting syndicate of a proposed issue of securities.

Level Debt Service—Principal and interest payments that together represent equal annual payments over the life of a loan. Principal may be serial maturities or sinking fund installments.

Liability—Debt or other obligations that must be satisfied in the future.

Limited Liability Bonds—Bonds that do not carry the full faith and credit pledge of a municipality.

Limited Tax Bond—A general obligation bond secured by the pledge of a specified tax or taxes.

Lipper General Municipal Bond Fund Index—The index measures the net asset values of 10 large municipal bond funds. The base of 100.00 was set on Dec. 31, 1980, when the index began.

List—The offering price of a bond; also used to connote a number of bonds out for the bid.

Locked Market—So-called when the bid and offered side of a quote are the same.

Lower Floater—A variable-rate bond with a put option enabling the holder to put the security back to the issuer.

M

M—Indicating that the number previous refers to thousands, i.e., 100M means 100,000.

Majors—Members of an underwriting syndicate who take down more than the average number of bonds; they rank below **managers.**

Managers—The chief members of an underwriting syndicate. The lead, senior or book-running manager handles the administration and allotment of a deal. The joint or co-managers comprise the remainder of the top members of a syndicate.

Mandatory Redemption Account—An account in the sinking fund into which an issuer makes deposits to be used to retire bonds as they are called.

Mark-Down—The difference between the cost of securities and their current price, in cases when the prices have fallen, or the amount received by a dealer selling securities to a third party for a customer.

Mark-to-Market—Taking the actual, market value of an inventory of securities.

Markup—1) An amount added to a security's cost in calculating its selling price, especially taking into account overhead and profit. 2) When a congressional committee drafts legislation. It is not a hearing, but a committee meeting to actually work out what will be in a bill. After the markup, the committee staff writes the bill.

Marketability—The ease or difficulty with which securities can be sold in the market.

Market Maker—A dealer or dealer bank which will make a bid or an offer at any time on a particular security.

Market Value—The price a security can command in the open market.

Master Resolution—The document stating the general terms under which an issuer may offer more than one series of bonds.

Matched Sales—Also known as reverse repurchase agreements, a method of lending money and taking securities as collateral; the lender later receives interest when the borrower buys back the securities.

Maturity—The date upon which principal value of a security is due and payable.

Maturity schedule—The schedule, with dates and amounts, of when principal becomes due.

Maturity Value—Par value.

Member Order—An order for part of a new issue, by a member of the underwriting syndicate.

Moral Obligation Bond—A municipal bond that is not backed by the full faith and credit of the issuer. The issuer has no legally enforceable obligation to pay.

Munifacts—The electronic news wire service of *The Bond Buyer* which transmits new offerings, proposed sales, runs, balances, news stories and market reports of interest to the municipal bond industry.

N

Negative Covenants—A promise in a bond covenant *not* to do something.

Negotiated Sale—A securities sale through an exclusive arrangement between the issuer and an underwriter or underwriting syndicate. This form of issuance provides one or more pricings, where the underwriters solicit potential buyers for the securities. Based on investor interest, the features of the securities may be altered to accommodate market demand or lack thereof. At the end of successful negotiations, the issue is awarded to the underwriters.

Net-Billing Agreements—Used by the Bonneville Power Administration to indirectly pay Pacific Northwest utilities for the costs of the Washington Public Power Supply System's nuclear projects 1, 2 and 3. Under the agreements, Bonneville gives each utility full credit for the WPPSS power on its other electricity purchases from the agency. All of the WPPSS 1, 2, and 3 participants are Bonneville customers.

Net Interest Cost—Represents the average coupon rate of a bond issue, weighted to reflect the term and adjusted for the premium or discount. It does not consider the time value of money ,as do Canadian, or true, interest cost *(which see)*. NIC = total coupon interest + discount (or - premium)/ bond years.

Net Price—Price paid for a bond by a retail customer.

Net Revenues—Gross revenues less operating and maintenance expenses. Net revenues are divided by debt service to get debt service ratio.

Nonlitigation Certificate—A written certificate which states that bonds, upon initial delivery, are free of legal complications.

Notes—Interest-bearing certificates of governments or corporations that come due in a shorter time than bonds. Treasury securities are notes if they mature in 10 years or less; municipal notes have maturities up to approximately one year.

Notice of Redemption—A publication announcing the issuer's intention to call outstanding bonds prior to maturity.

Notice of Sale—A printed document announcing and soliciting bids for the bonds or notes. It includes pertinent details of bidding requirements, date and time of sale, and a brief description of the purpose of the issue.

O

Object of Expenditure—Types of goods or services purchased or utilized by a municipality (i.e., salaries, utilities, supplies and capital outlays).

Odd Coupon—A coupon or interest payment that is longer or shorter than the normal six-month payment. It generally refers to the first interest payment of a new bond issue.

Odd Lot—A principal amount of bonds that is smaller than a normal trading block. Most traders consider an odd lot to be 100 bonds or 50 bonds.

Odd Lot Dealers—Bond dealers who purchase and sell bonds in lots smaller than $50,000.

Offer—The intention to sell securities at a given price or yield.

Offering Circular—A document that describes an issue of bonds that will be offered in the primary market. It consists of summaries of the deal's salient points.

Offering Price—The price at which a syndicate offers securities in a new issue to investors.

Official Advertisement—A municipality's announcement of an impending bond sale.

Official Circular—The document that sets forth the terms of the sale of a new municipal bond issue.

Official Notice—A letter distributed to prospective bidders announcing and describing an upcoming competitive municipal issue.

Official Statement—A document prepared by the issuer (or its financial adviser) that contains detailed information on the municipality and the security pledged to meet principal and interest; also known as a prospectus. Before the issue is priced it is known as the preliminary OS; afterwards, a final OS is distributed.

Open-End Fund—A mutual fund that does not have a fixed number of shares. An investor can sell back its shares at market value. In closed-end funds, there are a fixed number of shares.

Open-End Lien—A security provision in a revenue bond indenture that permits the issuer to issue additional securities which have an equal claim on pledged revenues, if it meets an additional bonds test.

Open-Ended Indenture—Permits an issuer to issue additional bonds or shares of bonds under the same indenture.

Operations and Maintenance Fund—A fund established in a revenue bond indenture that receives money to be used for meeting the costs of operating and maintaining the project.

Options Bonds—Bonds which the owner can tender on specified dates to the issuer in return for payment of the principal.

Order—A commitment made by a buyer to buy a stated number of bonds at the offered price.

Order Period—The time period after a new-issue competitive sale during which non-priority orders received from account members are allocated without consideration of the time of submission.

Original Issue Discount (OID) —The discount from par at which a new issue comes to market. The IRS has designated that the capital gain is tax free.

Original Proceeds—After payment of all issuance expenses, the net amount received by the issuer.

Overlapping Debt—The proportionate share of debt in addition to a community's own direct obligations, such as those issued by a county or school district in which it is located.

P

Par Bond—A bond selling at face value.

Par Option—A redemption provision that permits the issuer to call bonds at their face value.

Par Value—The principal amount of a bond that must be paid at maturity.

Parity Bonds—Separate bond issues which have the same lien against pledged revenues.

Partial Delivery—A delivery of bonds less than the total par value amount of bonds involved in the transaction.

Paying Agent—A bank or trust company that is appointed by a bond issuer to make principal and interest payments to bondholders.

Pay-As-You-Go-Basis—A policy of a municipality to pay for all capital outlays from current revenues, as opposed to borrowing.

Pay-As-You-Use Basis—Describes the financial policy of a municipality which finances its capital outlays by allocating costs among the users of each generation.

Payment Date—The date on which interest or principal and interest is due on a municipal bond.

Penalty Yield—A yield in excess of the par yield for a bond or other security.

Per Capita Debt—A municipality's outstanding debt divided by its population.

Performance Measures—Quantitative measures of results obtained through a governmental program or activity.

Philadelphia Plan—A plan under which coupon bonds are surrendered in exchange for registered bonds. The coupons are held by the paying agent until maturity or until used in reconversion of registered to coupon bonds.

Placement Ratio—The percentage of bonds from new issues that were sold during the week the issue came to market.

Pledged Revenues—The money promised to be put aside for the payment of debt service and other deposits required by the bond contract.

Point—One percent of par value. Since municipal dollar prices are quoted as a percentage of $1,000, a point is worth $10, regardless of the actual denomination of a security.

Polling the Account—A lead manager seeks the vote of syndicate members to determine syndicate policy on the disposal or sale of bonds.

Pollution Control Bond—A tax-exempt security issued to finance air or water pollution control facilities or sewage or solid waste facilities, pursuant to federal statutes and backed by the corporation or pollution control entity rather than the credit of the issuer.

Pool—A group of mortgages combined into a single security.

Pool Insurance—Insurance that guarantees principal and interest payments on the mortgages contained in a mortgage pool.

Position—A trading activity in which a dealer becomes long or short in a security.

Pot—The portion of bonds in a new offering that are set aside for discretionary distribution by the managers of a deal.

Preliminary Official Statement—The Official Statement in preliminary form. It does not contain pricing, yield or maturity information. Orders for securities may not be taken based on this document and a statement appearing in red confirms this fact. Because of this disclaimer, a POS is often called a "red herring."

Premium Bond—A bond whose price is above par.

Premium Call—A provision in the bond contract that permits a municipality to call securities at a price above par.

Pre-Sale Order—In a new-issue competitive underwriting, an order to purchase bonds given to the syndicate manager prior to the purchase of the deal.

Present Value—The current time value of a cash payment which is to be received in the future, allowing that an amount received today could be invested to earn interest for the period to future date.

Primary Market—The market for new-issue municipal securities.

Principal—The par value or face amount of a bond.

Principal Trade—A transaction in which a dealer purchases and takes ownership of bonds.

Private Placement—An original issue of bonds sold directly to an investor without a public offering.

Prior Issue—An outstanding issue of municipal bonds that possess a first or senior lien on pledged revenues, or are obligations being refinanced in a bond refunding.

Priority Provisions—The rules of an underwriting syndicate by which bond orders are honored. The general priority is pre-sale orders, followed by group net orders, designated orders and then member orders.

Pro forma—A projection of anticipated costs and revenues for a given project.

Proceeds—The money received by an issuer upon the deliver of bonds at a closing.

Production—The spread between the price at which a bond is purchased and the price at which the bond issue would be sold should all bonds be sold at the initial reoffering yield rates.

Pro-Rata-Share—A member's percentage of the total liability of an undivided underwriting account.

Protective Covenants—Bond contract agreements which impose duties on the issuer. They protect the bondholder by requiring segregation of funds, adequate debt service coverage, etc.

Provisional Rating—An estimate of what the credit quality of an issue is expected to be after an interim period.

Prudent Man Rule—A standard of conduct required of an individual who has a fiduciary responsibility.

Public Finance—That segment of the municipal industry that structures and markets bonds for issuers.

Public Housing Authority Bonds—Tax exempt bonds issued by local housing authorities to finance public housing guaranteed by the U.S. Government.

Public Sale—Competitive sale of a tax-exempt bond.

Public Securities Association—The national trade organization of municipal bond dealers and dealer banks.

Put Bonds—A bond that permits holders to tender the bonds to the trustee at a specified price and date.

Q

Qualified Bid—A secondary market bid that is subject to conditions (i.e.: an acceptable legal opinion).

Qualified Legal Opinion—A conditional legality of securities.

R

Ratings—Credit quality evaluation of bonds and notes made by independent rating services and brokerage firm analysts.

Rate Covenant—A bond indenture provision requiring rate charges necessary to meet annual debt service payments.

Realized Yield—A bond's return based on purchase price and the reinvestment of coupon payments at a stated reinvestment rate.

Reclamation—The returning of bonds that were accepted on settlement date due to a discovered deficiency (i.e., missing legal opinion).

Record Date—An assigned date prior to a registered bond's interest payment date which determines to whom the interest payment should be made. The party listed as the owner of the bond on the record date receives the interest payment.

Red Book—The *Bond Buyer's Directory of Municipal Bond Dealers of the United States,* which also contains a directory of bond counsel, financial advisers, credit enhancement firms and government officials.

Redemption—Also known as a **call,** it is the exchange of outstanding bonds for cash before maturity. The most common are optional redemption and mandatory redemptions.

Refunding—The underwriting of a new bond issue whose proceeds are used to redeem an outstanding issue.

Registered Bond—A bond whose owner's name is inscribed on the certificate. Interest payments go directly to the party named on the certificate.

Registrar—The party responsible for maintaining records on behalf of the issuer. It maintains the listing of the owners of registered bonds.

Regular Way Trade—A bond transaction where payment and delivery take place on the fifth business day after the trade date.

Reinvestment Risk—The risk a bondholder takes when reinvesting coupon payments. Interest rates may be lower when the owner seeks to reinvest income received from the security.

Reoffering—The yield or price scale at which a new issue is offered for sale.

Related Portfolio—A portfolio investing in municipal securities that is associated with a municipal securities dealer (i.e., a dealer bank's investment portfolio).

Reserve—An account, described in the bond indenture, used to indicate that a reserve fund is legally restricted for a specific purpose or not available for general appropriation and subsequent spending.

Retail—Individual investors, as opposed to institutional, or wholesale, buyers.

Revenue Anticipation Notes (RANs)—Notes issued in anticipation of nontax revenues, generally from other governmental entities (i.e., state aid to a school district).

Revenue Bonds—Bonds whose principal and interest are payable exclusively from earnings of a public enterprise.

Rollover—The issuance of new notes to retire outstanding notes.

Round Lot—An amount of bonds whose size is $100,000 par amount.

Run—In a new bond underwriting, the amount of bonds remaining in each maturity.

S

Secondary Market—The market for tax-exempt securities previously offered and sold, totaling roughly $850 billion.

Selling Group—A group of municipal dealers that assists in the distribution of a new issue of securities. These dealers are not members of the syndicate.

Senior Lien Bonds—Bonds having a prior claim or first claim on pledged revenues.

Serial Bonds—Municipal bonds whose principal is repaid in specific installments, generally once a year.

Settlement Date—The day on which there is delivery and payment for a bond.

Short Covering—The purchase of bonds previously sold short in order to deliver them and close the short position.

Short Position—An inventory position reflecting the sale of bonds that were not owned at the time of sale.

Short Sale—The sale of securities not owned at the time of sale.

Short-Term—Debt with a maturity under one year.

Sinking Fund—A fund established in a bond indenture that contains money that will be available to call bonds prior to maturity. The term sinking fund was derived from the concept of floating a bond issue. Accumulated money sinks bonds prior to maturity.

SLGS—Pronounced "Slugs," for State and Local Government Series. They are U.S. Government securities sold by the Treasury to municipalities which comply with arbitrage restrictions.

Special Assessment—A charge imposed against certain properties to defray part or all of the cost of a specific improvement or service deemed to primarily benefit those properties.

Special Assessment Bonds—Bonds payable from the proceeds of assessments imposed against properties which have been specially benefitted by the construction of public improvements.

Special Districts—A single purpose or local taxing district organized for a special purpose such as a road, sewer, irrigation or fire district.

Special Lien Bonds—Bonds whose indenture contains liens against particular pieces of property.

Special Tax Bond—A bond that is secured by a special tax, such as a liquor tax.

Split Ratings— Ratings assigned by more than one recognized rating service on a given municipality that differ substantially from each other.

Spread—The gross profit in an underwriting.

Stickering—The act of amending the information provided in an official statement on a new issue.

Straight Serial Bonds—Serial bonds in which the annual installments of bond principal are about equal.

"Street" Name—The registration of bonds in the name of a dealer or other third party instead of the owner, usually for custodial purposes.

Strip Call—The redemption of bonds of an issue by calling a portion of each maturity.

Super Sinker—A term maturity, generally found in a single-family mortgage bond issue. The bonds in this maturity will be called from prepayment proceeds before any other term maturity.

Swap—Selling one issue and buying another to effect a change in yield to maturity, coupon or maturity.

Syndicate—A group of investment bankers who join together to bid on a new bond issue.

Syndicate Letter—A contract which binds underwriters together.

Syndicate Restrictions—Contractual obligations of underwriting members relating to distribution, price limitations and market transactions.

T

Take-and-Pay, Take-or-Pay (contracts). Used to guarantee payments for financing of new projects, especially power plants. Take-and-pay contracts obligate the backers to pay debt service if the plant is capable of producing any power; take-or-pay contracts require the backers to pay regardless of whether or not the plant ever produces power.

Takedown — The discount off list price available to a member of an underwriting group when he purchases bonds from the syndicate for retail distribution.

Taxable Equivalent Yield—The yield an investor would have to obtain on a taxable corporate or U.S. government bond to match the same after-tax yield on a municipal bond.

Tax and Revenue Anticipation Notes (TRANs)--Short-term debt that will be retired with taxes and other government revenues to be collected at a later date.

Tax Anticipation Notes (TANs) — Short-term debt that will be retired with taxes to be collected at a later date.

Tax Increment Bond—A bond secured by the excess dollars of specific taxes after taking into account the historic monetary yield of such taxes.

Tax Liens—Claims which governments have upon properties until levied taxes against them have been paid.

Tax Limit—The maximum rate of taxation which a local government may levy.

Tender Offer—A proposal by an issuer to buy back its bonds at a specific price.

TENR—Tax Exempt Note Rate. Bankers Trust Co.'s weekly interest rate on its variable note deals.

Term Bonds—Applies to a municipal issue having all or the bulk of the bonds maturing on a single date.

Thin Market—A condition for obscure bonds in which trading is low and spreads are wide.

Tight Market—A condition for active bonds where volume is great and spreads are narrow.

Tombstone—An advertisement placed by underwriters describing the terms of a new municipal offering.

Total Debt—Direct debt plus overlapping and underlying debt.

Trade Date—The date when a bond transaction is executed.

Traders—Secondary market operators who purchase and sell bond positions.

Transfer—The process of changing the name of the owner on a registered security.

Transfer Agent—The entity which performs the transfer function for registered municipal securities.

True Interest Cost (TIC)—Also known as **Canadian Interest Cost,** a method of computing interest cost for new issues involving discounted present value.

True Valuation—Market price of real estate on an issuer's tax roll.

Trustee—A bank designated to act in a fiduciary capacity for the benefit of bondholders in enforcing the terms of the bond contract.

Two-Sided Market—The bid and offer prices at which a broker-dealer's bond traders would be willing to effect a transaction in a security.

U

Underlying Debt—The debt of smaller municipal units within a given government's jurisdiction.

Underwriting—The process of purchasing a new issue of municipal bonds from the issuer and offering the bonds for sale to investors.

Underwriter—The dealer who buys the new issue of securities from the issuer and offers the bonds for sale to investors.

Underwriting Agreement—See **Syndicate Letter.**

Underwriting Spread—The dollar amount difference between the price at which bonds are bought from the issuer and the price at which they are reoffered to the investor.

Undivided Account—An underwriting agreement in which each member of the group is liable for any unsold portion of the issue by the other underwriters.

Unexpended Proceeds Call—An extraordinary redemption feature often found in single-family housing issues. If proceeds of the bond issue cannot be placed in mortgages due to lack of demand by a certain date, bonds are called from the unexpended proceeds.

Unit Investment Trust—A self-liquidating, closed-end, fixed portfolio of bonds selected to meet a specific investment objective.

Unlimited Tax Bond—A bond secured by taxes that are not limited in rate or amount.

Upgrade—An improved rating by a rating service.

V

Variable Rate—A tax-exempt security whose interest rate periodically changes. The rate is usually based on some formula. It is also known as a "floater."

Visible Supply—The total dollar value of new securities expected to be offered over the next 30 days.

W

Warrant—A certificate giving the holder the right to purchase a bond at a specific price during a certain time period.

When Issued —A conditional offering of bonds made subject to their actual delivery to the underwriter.

Workable—A bid price at which a dealer states its willingness to purchase bonds from another dealer. A dealer giving a workable is free to revise its bid if market conditions change.

Y

Yield—The annual rate of return on an investment expressed as percentage.

Yield to Average Life—The yield derived when the average life date is substituted for the maturity rate of a bond.

Yield to Call—Uses the call date instead of the maturity date and the call price rather than face value to determine the yield.

Yield Curve—A graph that shows the relationship of one point in time between yields and maturities of the same bonds.

Yield to Maturity—Total return on a bond, taking into consideration its coupon, length of maturity and dollar price.

Yield to Put Option—The rate of return to the bondholder, assuming that the bond is put back to the issuer on the put date.

Yield Pickup—The gain in yield to an investor resulting from a swap of lower for higher coupon yields.

Z

Zero Coupon Bonds—Bonds sold at a discount rate that have no coupons attached.

Index

About the Authors

George J. Marlin, a fixed income portfolio manager is a 15 year veteran of the municipal bond industry. He served as a legislative assistant to several New York State legislators. During New York City's 1975 financial crisis, he was executive director of the Former Police Officers Association, an organization that represented the city's laid-off police officers.

Mr. Marlin is general editor of the *Collected Works of G.K. Chesterton* (Ignatius Press) and editor of *The Quotable Chesterton, More Quotable Chesterton* and *The Quotable Fulton Sheen* (Doubleday). His articles have appeared in numerous periodicals, including *National Review, Crisis, The Chesterton Review, Fidelity, Credit Markets, Reflections, MuniWeek* and *The Wanderer.* A frequent contributor to *The Bond Buyer*, Mr. Marlin has written extensively on New York's finances and politics.

Joe Mysak is managing editor of *The Bond Buyer*, where he has worked since January 1981. He began on the copy desk, and worked as a general assignment reporter, a beat reporter covering New York municipal issuers, the National Association of State Treasurers, and bond insurers, and as assistant managing editor.

Prior to joining *The Bond Buyer*, Mr. Mysak was an editor for the Access Daily News Intelligence Service. He also worked for *More* magazine, the journalism review.

Mr. Mysak's interests extend well beyond the municipal bond market. He freelances extensively, and is a contributing editor of both *National Review* and *The American Spectator*.

His work has appeared in *The New York Times*, where he has had feature pieces on Winston Churchill's country seat, Chartwell, and on the White House of the Confederacy in Richmond, Va. His work has also appeared in *Barron's*, and his book reviews in *The Wall Street Journal*. Mr. Mysak is an associate editor of *The Collected Works of G.K. Chesterton*, a member of the International Churchill Society and the H.L. Mencken Society, and serves on the board of trustees of the Fulton J. Sheen Society.